The American History Series

SERIES EDITORS

John Hope Franklin, *Duke University*
A. S. Eisenstadt, *Brooklyn College*

Glenn Porter
DIRECTOR EMERITUS
HAGLEY MUSEUM AND LIBRARY

The Rise of Big Business 1860–1920

THIRD EDITION

HARLAN DAVIDSON, INC.
WHEELING, ILLINOIS 60090-6000

Library of Congress Cataloging-in-Publication Data

Porter, Glenn.
   The rise of big business, 1860–1920 / Glenn Porter.—3rd ed.
     p.cm. — (The American history series)
   Includes bibliographical references and index.
   ISBN-13: 978-0-88295-240-6 (alk. paper)
   ISBN-10: 0-88295-240-4 (alk. paper)
   1. Big business—United States—History. I. Title. II. Series: American history series (Wheeling, Ill.)
   HD2356.U5P67 2006
   338.6'44'0973—dc22
                     2005014633

Cover photograph: "The Hand of Man," by Alfred Stieglitz, 1902. Photogravure Medium, Image: 24.1 x 31.8 cm (9 1/2 x 12 1/2 in.) *Courtesy The J. Paul Getty Museum, Los Angeles. © The J. Paul Getty Museum.*

Manufactured in the United States of America
09 08 07 06 05 1 2 3 4 5 VP

FOREWORD

Every generation writes its own history for the reason that it sees the past in the foreshortened perspective of its own experience. This has surely been true of the writing of American history. The practical aim of our historiography is to give us a more informed sense of where we are going by helping us understand the road we took in getting where we are. As the nature and dimensions of American life are changing, so too are the themes of our historical writing. Today's scholars are hard at work reconsidering every major aspect of the nation's past: its politics, diplomacy, economy, society, recreation, mores and values, as well as status, ethnic, race, sexual, and family relations. The lists of series titles that appear on the inside covers of this book will show at once that our historians are ever broadening the range of their studies.

The aim of this series is to offer our readers a survey of what today's historians are saying about the central themes and aspects of the American past. To do this, we have invited to write for the series only scholars who have made notable contributions to the respective fields in which they are working. Drawing on primary and secondary materials, each volume presents a factual and narrative account of its particular subject, one that affords readers a basis for perceiving its larger dimensions and importance. Conscious that readers respond to the closeness and immediacy of a subject, each of our authors seeks to restore the past as an actual present, to revive it as a living reality. The individuals and groups who figure in the pages of our books appear as real people who once were looking for survival and fulfillment. Aware that historical subjects are often matters of controversy, our authors present their own findings and conclusions. Each volume closes with an extensive critical essay on the writings of the major authorities on its particular subject.

The books in this series are designed for use in both basic and advanced courses in American history, on the undergraduate and graduate levels. Such a series has a particular value these days, when the format of American history courses is being altered to accommodate a greater diversity of reading materials. The series offers a number of distinct advantages. It extends the dimensions of regular course work. Going well beyond the confines of the textbook, it makes clear that the study of our past is, more than the student might otherwise understand, at once complex, profound, and absorbing. It presents that past as a subject of continuing interest and fresh investigation. The work of experts in their respective fields, the series, moreover, puts at the disposal of the reader the rich findings of historical inquiry. It invites the reader to join, in major fields of research, those who are pondering anew the central themes and aspects of our past. And it reminds the reader that in each successive generation of the ever-changing American adventure, men and women and children were attempting, as we are now, to live their lives and to make their way.

John Hope Franklin
A. S. Eisenstadt

CONTENTS

PREFACE
TO THE THIRD EDITION

The fundamental changes in the American economy and its business system in the closing decades of the nineteenth century and the first years of the twentieth continue to fascinate and engage historians, economists, and sociologists. Those revolutionary shifts were intimately linked to transformations in the nation's culture and its politics. This made the Gilded Age and the early twentieth century one of the most critical periods in American history.

The accumulation of notable new scholarship on the social context and consequences of economic change in that era has caused me to recast numerous portions of this book, particularly in the third chapter and the bibliographical essay. My views about the fundamental characteristics of big business and the basic forces that called it into being, however, have remained substantially as they were. Although many disagreements persist about the precise economic consequences and motivations of the actors, most historians and economists roughly agree on the central shifts in technologies and markets that called forth big business. Recent scholars have, however, produced important new work on the changing cultural values and sensibilities of Americans living through that time, on women and business, on the ties between the emerging corporations and many other institutions in American life, as well as new considerations of the nature of competition among giant firms, the beginnings of modern advertising and the department store, and a number of other related topics. Increasingly, historians are looking beyond the traditional issues of regulation and the political dimensions of the emergence of concentrated enterprise. These new perspectives have led me to extend the treatment of the impact of the rise of big business. This edition expands the consideration of the corporation on social history, especially the history of women.

In a real sense, modern America was launched in the era considered in this book, for the nation, though sorely tried by the stresses, changed dramatically in its accommodation to the revolutionary new institution. By the time of World War I, the general outlines of that accommodation and the powerful linkages between business and other elements in American society were reasonably clear.

The particular kind of business institution whose rise is traced in the following pages did not triumph in all sectors of the economy by any means, nor did it represent the end of the story of the evolution of corporate enterprise. As circumstances shifted in the decades after 1920, other forms emerged in reaction to further change, the only constant in history. But the pioneer form of large-scale enterprise was a powerful and disruptive institution, one that influenced deeply the course of American history.

Whether the coming of those giant corporate organizations was for the good or ill of humankind is for each reader to determine. What is beyond doubt is that the rise of big business was central to the transformation of life in the United States of America for much of the twentieth century. I hope that this book may contribute to a better understanding of the structure and functions of the large corporation, how and why it arose and spread, and some of the ways in which it had such a revolutionary impact.

Glenn Porter
Director Emeritus
Hagley Museum and Library

CHAPTER ONE

What is Big Business?

In the years framed by the Civil War and World War I, Americans encountered a revolutionary new institution, the giant corporation. It arose first in the railroads, then in many manufacturing industries, then in the distribution of numerous goods, services, and information. It came as a central part of what Robert Wiebe called the search for order, in his influential 1967 book of that name. What had been a fundamentally rural, agrarian nation composed of what Wiebe considered "island communities" and small businesses, emerged as an urbanized, modern, "distended" nation dominated by a new middle class in business and the professions. That national transformation was many sided and complex, but its most significant new institution was the large-scale business enterprise.

Big businesses did not appear everywhere in the United States economy of the late nineteenth and early twentieth centuries. Numerous sectors remained in the hands of small and middling enterprises. Nevertheless, the large corporation came to dominate many industries in what Robert Averitt in *The Dual Economy* (1968) termed the *center economy*. (Averitt's center firms resembled the big businesses described here; smaller businesses he termed *periphery firms*.) The coming of the giant enterprises of the Gilded Age had profound effects on American society, on politics, on the law, and on many aspects of our national life.

Adjusting to, and accepting, these powerful new actors on the national stage was painful and difficult. Although they brought many positive changes, they represented concentrated wealth and power on an unprecedented scale. They seemed to threaten democracy itself. They assaulted the older, rural, republican America in fundamental ways. Many citizens found them deeply troubling, even frightening. As social historian Stuart Blumin wrote in the *Cambridge Economic History of the United States* (2000), "the late nineteenth century's rapid centralization of capitalist institutions was an earthquake that shook the ground on which nearly all Americans stood." Blumin also noted the cool judgment issued by journalist Walter Lippmann in 1914 that the old order had become "doomed by the great organization that had come into the world." This little book seeks to explain how and why big business, the principal instrument of that "great organization," came into being.

The rise of big business stood at the core of a broad range of changes in American life, shifts in other institutions, and in the very values and perceptions through which citizens understood themselves and their relation to the world around them. From the nation's beginnings through the middle decades of the nineteenth century, wrote William Leach in *Land of Desire* (1993), "most American white men were self-employed voters, owners of landed property, and producers of foodstuffs and raw materials" for their families and for a wider market. Wealth lay mostly in land, and virtue lay in producing and in saving, more than in consuming. Although individualism had always been a powerful force in the United States, there were also strong, long-standing notions of the importance of community and what Leach termed "civic well-being." That older America, largely republican and dominated by the ideal of the individual as producer, was swept away during the years that brought big business. It did not pass away without struggle, and it never disappeared entirely. But by the time of World War I, it had largely been replaced by a new consumer culture. "The cardinal features of this culture," Leach noted, "were acquisition and consumption as the means of achieving happiness; the cult of the new; the democratization of desire; and money value as the predominant measure of all value in society." All these were characteristic of a wide and deep sea of changes that Alan Trachtenberg called the incorporation of America, in his 1982 book of that name.

While taking note of many of the social and cultural consequences of the coming of large-scale corporations, the focus in this book will remain on the central economic institution that produced those revolutionary changes. By examining the core reasons for the appearance of big business and its subsequent spread, we can understand better the nature and evolution of our own society. Most Americans now clearly consider the existence of big business a normal and natural part of their lives, like the certainty of taxes and the four seasons. Many citizens, of course, remain deeply concerned about abuses of power by large corporations, the ominous environmental effects of unbridled growth, and the dangers posed by the often intimate connections between business and government. Nevertheless, it is clear that the American political process long ago accepted the fact of the existence of big business, that large-scale enterprises are hardly likely to be destroyed or fundamentally altered via political action, though their behavior will continue to be constrained and influenced by political and social criticisms. This acceptance was not always so clear.

Throughout our national history, Americans shaped much of their politics around one or another form of the struggle over big business and its influence. The lineage of ideas about the evils of large-scale business in the United States goes back at least as far as Thomas Jefferson. Later, Andrew Jackson and his followers molded an era around the fight to destroy the "monster" Bank of the United States and its influence. Both the populist and progressive movements, though extremely complex, were ultimately rooted in a deep reluctance to accept the rise of big business without protest. After an apparent national accommodation with the new economic order in the 1920s, the New Deal era witnessed what may well have been the Indian summer of any genuine widespread interest in antitrust movements.

Our earlier political conflicts about business, like most political clashes, were couched in vague terms. Few people were specific about what they meant by *big business, the trusts, combinations,* or how to control this phenomenon and correct its evils. In addition, the opposition to large-scale business often was mixed with a confused array of related but distinct ideas such as the persistent idealization of rural, agrarian civilization—what Richard Hofstadter in *The Age of Reform* (1955) called the "agrarian myth." Most Americans of the late nineteenth and early twentieth centuries witnessed in confusion and doubt the passing of the older society whose businesses had generally been small, local affairs.

The coming of giant corporations was profoundly unsettling, for the process not only altered the way of life of the majority of people, but it seemed to call into question many of the ideas and values by which Americans had defined themselves and their nation. The belief in competition and democracy, the goals of producing and saving, the idea that individuals could rise through their own efforts to wealth and power—or at least to something close to self-sufficiency—all seemed overshadowed by the giant corporations whose influence came to be felt in virtually every city and town across the land. Of the many changes that have occurred in our history, few have made such a deep and lasting difference as the emergence of an industrial, urban, consumer civilization and its characteristic institution, the large corporation. Until the 1950s, however, historians had talked a great deal about the opposition to business but had provided relatively little in the way of thoughtful generalizations about the process by which big business actually arose.

Historical work on the coming of giant corporations reflected the rather paradoxical way in which Americans responded to large-scale enterprise itself. At the same time that the American people were deeply troubled by the rise of big business, they were also eagerly embracing it. No other country in the world made antitrust such a major political issue, and none has exhibited the long-running tradition of institutionalized concern about big business that has marked the United States. Paradoxically, few if any nations have created so many giant firms so quickly as the United States. Americans have always admired mammoth economic organizations while at the same time fearing them, and the treatment of the rise of big business by American historians long reflected these conflicting popular views.

For many years, most historical assessments of the rise of big business were either emotionally slanted attacks on the "robber barons" or else attempts to refute such interpretations by focusing on the positive aspects in the coming of large-scale enterprises (such contributions as greater productive efficiency). The first group of historians usually coupled a "liberal" or "progressive" political preference with a view of history in which the rise of big business was seen as the inevitable result of capitalism's continuous tendency toward the concentration of capital and production into larger and larger units. "If society is founded on the idea that property belongs to the strongest," Henry Demarest Lloyd argued in *Wealth Against Commonwealth* (1894), "these will sooner or later get all the property, by bargains or by battles according to 'the spirit of the age.'" Some of the leading contributions to the robber baron school of historiography, such as Matthew Josephson, *The Robber Barons* (1934), demonstrated an appreciation of the varieties and complexities of history by acknowledging the role of factors such as entrepreneurship, technology, and plain good luck in shaping the coming of big business. Rather than lingering on explanations of the coming of big business, however, such historical works usually featured moral denunciations of the greed and ruthlessness of big business leaders, questioning the appropriateness of the wealth and power that society conferred on a relative few. Invoking the American ideals of political and economic democracy, Josephson denounced the "new nobility" whose members "organize and exploit . . . farmers and workers into harmonious corps of producers . . . only in the name of an uncontrolled appetite for private profit."

The opposing interpretation of the period was, for many years, that the business giants had made positive contributions by bringing greater efficiency and organization to the economy. This approach came to be known as the "industrial statesmen" view. By looking at events from the perspective of the business giants, these historians naturally came to see history in terms that made virtually all business behavior seem reasonable, even praiseworthy. Sometimes this process of revisionism all but turned the robber baron approach on its head, as in Julius Grodinsky's *Jay Gould* (1957) and Maury Klein's *Life and Legend of Jay Gould* (1986). Matthew Josephson had called Gould (an unscrupulous railroad promoter and stock manipulator of the 1870s and 1880s) "Mephistopheles." Klein's portrait of Gould was highly positive, and Grodinsky believed that Gould's schemes "performed a service to society" by encouraging competition. One could choose a political preference, observe the era from the standpoint of the large businesses or "the public interest," and conclude whether Andrew Carnegie, John D. Rockefeller, James B. Duke, and the others were robber barons or industrial statesmen.

The historical treatment of the coming of big business was part of the larger, twentieth-century trend toward "progressive history." Liberal historians interpreted American history as a series of conflicts between the forces of good (fighting for greater democracy and a more nearly equal distribution of wealth) and the opposing forces of conservatism (fighting to maintain the status quo). This interpretive tradition stood dominant in America at least until the late 1950s. Dissenters (usually called "revisionists") merely had a different set of political views; they did not alter the prevailing view of history as a moral struggle.

Much of the later historical work seriously eroded the progressive view of history. The "consensus" historians of the 1950s and 1960s emphasized what they saw as the relatively narrow range of political and social disagreement in the American past, and they undermined the progressive historians by pointing out the uglier sides of various reform movements, such as anti-Semitism, racism, and nativism. Thereafter the New Left historians broke completely with the progressive historians' admiration for the liberal reform movements, denouncing the reformers for failing to bring more fundamental changes. Gabriel Kolko's *The Triumph of Conservatism* (1963), for example, painted the progressive movement as an essentially conservative phenomenon heavily influenced by business.

In recent decades, many American historians have found broad, unifying, interpretive structures less attractive and have turned to a mosaic of topics, with an emphasis on the role of race, class, and gender. Some cultural historians, on the other hand, have embraced new overarching themes about broad changes in values, even about what they see as shifts in consciousness itself, flowing from the incorporation of America and its consumer culture.

The decline of progressive history, and perhaps a spreading dissatisfaction with traditional American liberalism as an organizing social philosophy, sent historians looking for new ways of doing history. Some turned to quantification and sought through voting analyses, demographic data, and econometric models to produce a new history that would qualify as a truly scientific "social science." Others, drawing on sociology, organization theory, and (to a lesser extent) economics, attempted to analyze process and structure without so explicitly passing moral judgments on the individuals of the past. This kind of work was particularly evident in business history. The scholarship of Alfred D. Chandler, Jr., came in the last few decades to dominate our understanding of the history of large business organizations, not only in the United States but throughout the developed world. In a body of scholarship ranging from the late 1950s through his two major books, *Strategy and Structure* (1962), and *The Visible Hand* (1977), Chandler argued that improvements in technology were the driving forces in explaining the rise of big business. The form and function of a business enterprise, in Chandler's view, was shaped by the nature and complexity of the tasks it performed rather than by the morality of its masters. Implicitly, this way of looking at history accepts the premise that the overriding, legitimate purpose of any business is to make a profit by employing resources productively over long periods. Further, it assumes that we can learn more about the history of business if we focus on understanding patterns of organizational structure and function, as well as changing forms of competition, than if we emphasize moral judgments about the motives of individuals or seek to analyze the personalities of heroic individuals. Some recent scholars, as explained in the Bibliographical Essay, have found numerous flaws in Chandler's fundamentally positive account of the coming of large-scale business and its subsequent evolution. Nevertheless, our present understanding of the coming of dominant corporations remains shaped principally by Chandler's work. We have suggestive new approaches in business and economic history, and some intriguing broad interpretations in the realm of values and culture, but no comprehensive, alternative synthesis has yet emerged to explain the rise of big business itself.

We can deepen our understanding of the appearance of large-scale enterprises, however, by looking beyond the technological and institutional changes that made the large corporation possible, acknowledging the role of politics as well as of markets, social stresses and national doubts, as well as changing transportation and communication networks, production processes, legal environments, and financial institutions. The large corporation, like most individuals and many institutions, behaved according to a mix of motives, and it had both positive and negative consequences. By exploring these and similar questions, we may be able to gain more insight into this important part of American history than by approaching the topic seeking to assign blame or praise.

Within the course of only half a century or so, the American economy, society, and polity were transformed by the rise of big business and the "earthquake" it represented. How did an institution barely present in the 1860s come to be the predominant economic form in many vital sectors of the economy by the end of the second decade of the twentieth century? This book seeks to answer that question.

The essential first step is to be clear about the meaning of the term *big business*. The principal purpose of this first chapter, therefore, is to provide a general definition of the nature and functions of big business; the creature will at least be surrounded if not completely subdued. It is important to understand the differences between this brand of large-scale enterprise and the smaller business firms common in the United States before the last half of the nineteenth century.

There are a great many kinds of businesses operating in the American economy. Major examples include: agriculture; forestry; mining; information processing; construction; transportation; communications; utilities; wholesale and retail trade; finance; service industries such as repair facilities and legal, medical, and educational businesses; and the operations of various governmental agencies. When Americans think of big business, however, they usually think of the large corporations engaged primarily in manufacturing or retailing—General Motors, Exxon, General Electric, Wal★Mart, and so on. In recent decades they have also come to think of the leaders in information technology such as Microsoft, as well as the many foreign-based giants that play a highly visible and growing role here—Toyota, Siemens, Sony, Mitsubishi, Michelin, BMW, and others. In the era considered in this book, when people spoke of big businesses they usually had in mind three kinds of enterprises in particular: railroads, manufacturing companies, and banks. The individuals who, for a time, dominated such businesses—the Vanderbilts, Harrimans, Rockefellers, Carnegies, Fords, Morgans, and others—symbolized the giant firms that were changing the economy. Although other kinds of businesses, both then and later, exhibited some of the characteristics of big business, it was the "rise" of large-scale companies in those three areas (especially in railroads and manufacturing) that signaled the coming of a new economic order in the land.

Indeed, railroads and manufacturing are the industries with which most of this book will deal.

Big business refers, at least here, to a particular kind of institution through which goods and services were financed, produced, and distributed. A big business was a very different economic creation from the businesses of colonial and early national days. It was structured and it functioned in new ways.

Most enterprises Americans considered big businesses exhibited distinctive features. One obvious characteristic of large-scale enterprises was that they embodied much larger pools of capital than had the businesses of earlier days. In contrast, the typical business establishment of the first half of the nineteenth century was financed by a single person or several people bound together in a partnership. As such, it represented the personal wealth of a very few persons. Most manufacturing enterprises (with exceptions such as some textile mills and iron furnaces) were quite small, involving little in the way of physical plants or expensive machinery. It was relatively easy to get into business, for the initial costs of going into trade or simple manufacturing were within the reach of many citizens. Business failures were frequent, but there was little social or even economic stigma attached to having failed unless the bankrupt person was thought dishonest; stupidity, but not deception, was repeatedly forgivable. Corporations were rare and business had a very personal tone. The fact that it was easy to enter business nurtured the belief that the society was open and fluid, that this was a land of opportunity. The goods most people bought were made and sold by small businesses, and because the capital requirements for most businesses were small, most white males could reasonably dream of owning and operating their own establishments. A great many people in antebellum America, it seemed, were in business, if only in a small way. "What most astonishes me in the United States," Alexis de Tocqueville recalled of his visit in the 1830s, "is not so much the marvelous grandeur of some undertakings, as the innumerable multitudes of small ones."

The investment represented by many of the late-nineteenth-century corporations was vastly larger than even the grandest undertakings of the antebellum years. The buildings and machines of the later enterprises were numerous and costly. The capital needed to build, maintain, and operate the many factories, warehouses, offices, distribution facilities, and other accouterments of big business was enormous. It was almost impossible to create and run such institutions without gathering money from many people. The investment represented by early giant enterprises such as Standard Oil, American Tobacco, Swift & Company, and the various large railroads such as the Pennsylvania and the Baltimore & Ohio (B&O) amounted to many millions of dollars. For example, the carefully researched study of Standard Oil by two sympathetic revisionist historians (Ralph and Muriel Hidy's *Pioneering in Big Business, 1882–1911,* 1955) showed the company's net book value in 1910 to be in excess of $600 million. And when U.S. Steel was created in 1901, the aspect of the news that most amazed and impressed contemporaries was the fact that the firm was capitalized at more than a billion dollars. By way of comparison, the capital requirements of even the largest of antebellum manufacturers— the textile companies—was seldom more than a million dollars, and those of the vast majority of firms engaged in factory production before 1860 were very much smaller. The coming of giant corporations soon altered the old assumption that almost anyone could go into business and have some chance of succeeding as well as the next person. Ordinary citizens who sat around planning the creation of, for instance, another U.S. Steel in 1901 with the savings and credit of a few friends would surely have been thought lunatics.

Another important difference between small and large businesses was related to the scale of capital needs just discussed. This related distinction lay in the different nature of capital requirements and costs for large and small firms. A business needed two kinds of capital, fixed and working, and it encountered two kinds of costs, fixed (or constant) and operating (or variable). Put in a highly simplified way, fixed capital or assets were those represented by a company's land, buildings, and machinery; working capital was the money needed to run the business once it was in operation. Fixed (or constant) costs were those borne by the firm whether or not it was producing—costs such as interest charges on the fixed capital, taxes, and so on. Operating costs, on the other hand, comprised salaries, wages, raw materials, and any costs directly associated with production, distribution, and transportation. The small manufacturers of the first half of the nineteenth century found that their yearly operating costs were very high, often exceeding the initial expense of the land and physical plant. That is, working capital was much more important than was fixed capital for most early businesses. Merchants and small artisan-entrepreneurs had even less in the way of fixed capital and fixed costs. When a depression or a recession struck, it was not hard for a firm to ride it out simply by closing down temporarily and sending the employees home. "When an article was produced by a small manufacturer, employing, probably at his own home, two or three journeymen and an apprentice or two," Andrew Carnegie wrote in an 1889 magazine article, "it was an easy matter for him to limit or even to stop production." Because the physical plant did not represent much capital, it did not disturb an owner greatly to see it lying idle. Even if the money tied up in the idle factory were invested in securities or loaned to others, the interest it would have earned would not have been a great amount. Because the operating costs were so high and the constant costs relatively low, antebellum firms had considerable control over when and under what circumstances they would continue to do business.

Because of the scale and scope of their operations, the situation for big businesses was quite different. A central part of the story of the coming of large-scale enterprise was advances in science and technology, which made possible mass production and mass distribution in many industries and brought about new processes in the production of metals, petroleum, chemicals, electrical products, automobiles, and other items. Most of the new giant firms used complex technologies and many manufacturing plants, and they did so because the new production techniques made it possible to turn out huge quantities of goods at a much lower cost per unit.

The coming of the complex new technologies and the multisite, multifunction companies had significant effects on the behavior of the firms involved. The many factories, mills, refineries, warehouses, blast furnaces, assembly lines, and distribution outlets represented enormous amounts of capital, so these firms experienced substantially higher constant costs than had their antebellum predecessors. This made it more costly to cease production when business turned bad. The extremely intricate interconnections between the various parts of a far-flung modern enterprise also made it more difficult to plan and coordinate downturns in production. Start-up costs were substantial, and market share might be lost to competitors during the slowdown. "As manufacturing is carried on today [1889]," the steel king Carnegie argued in the *North American Review*, "in enormous establishments with five or ten millions of dollars of capital invested, . . . it costs the manufacturer much less to run at a loss per ton or per yard than to check his production. Stoppage would be serious indeed. . . . Therefore the article is produced for months [or] for years . . . without profit or without interest on capital." Indeed, many of the new industries depended on high-volume, relatively steady levels of operation to achieve their low costs per unit of output. This made them inclined to keep the production lines rolling, which in turn contributed to the persistent decline in prices that marked the latter half of the nineteenth century and heightened business concerns about what many saw as excessive competition.

Some of the most important changes in the behavior of businesses after the coming of large-scale enterprise resulted from the fact that once a few large firms controlled an industry, barriers to entry by new competitors became much higher. The old assumptions that one could enter manufacturing or other lines of business relatively easily passed away in many industries. In addition, the few firms that rose to dominate any one industry no longer competed primarily on the basis of price but in other ways. The costs of building giant plants, financing extensive distribution networks, establishing new national brands of consumer goods, creating costly research and development arms—all characteristic of many big businesses—meant that giant firms enjoyed more protection from competition than businesses had experienced earlier. Operating behind barriers to entry assured more stability and predictability, which had been a central objective behind the creation of many giant businesses.

None of this, however, indicated the disappearance of change in the business world or the vanishing of the power of the market. Even large firms in industries consisting of only a few corporations remained subject to the threat of new technologies arising outside the established firms, to foreign competition, and to competition from substitute goods or services. Although many of the new giant enterprises had a newfound influence over prices, the pressure or potential of market challenges kept competitive pricing alive, at least in the long run. Even after the raising of significant barriers to entry, it was, as Naomi Lamoureaux skeptically noted in her 1985 study, *The Great Merger Movement in American Business, 1895–1904,* the "conventional wisdom of the economics profession that the economy" remained "'workably competitive.'" But the competitive behavior of large firms was clearly different than that of smaller ones in lesser industries.

These comments about the capital needs, complex costs, and competitive environments of a big business point to another related and important difference between it and the smaller institutions of the more distant past. That distinction was the altered nature of ownership. The business enterprises of the early United States were usually owned by one or by several individuals, often bound together by ties of kinship and marriage. This familial aspect of antebellum business traced its lineage back to the earliest colonial days, as Bernard Bailyn's investigation of *The New England Merchants in the Seventeenth Century* (1955) indicated. Normally the owners of a business were also its managers. They knew intimately the needs and mode of operation of their businesses. They brought their sons, nephews, or talented in-laws into their firms to learn the details of the business, and when a firm's management changed, so often did its ownership. Almost all antebellum businesses fit this pattern, from the smallest storekeepers to the richest and most powerful families, such as the Browns in Rhode Island and the Hancocks,

Lowells, and Appletons in Massachusetts. Because of the intensely personal nature of ownership and control, these early businesses often died with the passing of the owner or the lack of interest or absence of talent among the surviving members in the family. The handful of owners bore responsibility for making the key decisions for the business and for providing the entrepreneurial vision and drive that guided its survival and growth. For that reason, the type of business that prevailed before the era of large corporations was termed the *entrepreneurial firm* by Louis Galambos and Joseph Pratt in *The Rise of the Corporate Commonwealth* (1988).

Big business functioned with another method of ownership altogether. As economists Adolf A. Berle and Gardiner C. Means pointed out early in the 1930s in a book later enshrined as "a classic study," *The Modern Corporation and Private Property* (1933), a hallmark of the modern business enterprise was its separation of ownership and control. Because huge pools of capital were necessary to launch a large concern, ownership usually had to be distributed among a great many people, and that in turn meant that the owner-entrepreneur commonly had no place in this new kind of enterprise. As the corporation replaced the partnership as the organizational form for many firms around the turn of the century, the number of owners (shareholders) grew so large that multiple owners had to turn over control of the business to one person or a few individuals. And as the complexity of management grew, the corporations eventually came to be run by professionals who had very little or no ownership at all in the firms they piloted. It became increasingly rare, especially after the beginning of the twentieth century, for the management of a major firm to remain in the hands of a single family. William Miller, in a study of the leaders of giant business enterprises in the period from 1901 to 1910 (published in a collection of essays, *Men in Business*, 1962), found that the majority were either managers who had risen through the company bureaucracy or outside professionals with special skills, such as lawyers. Once ownership was widely spread and management became the job of skilled professionals, the firm was freed from its old dependence on the money, talent, and health of any one person or small circle. It could become virtually an immortal institution, easily surviving the deaths of owners and the onset of incompetence or disinterest in any single family. The rise of big business inevitably brought with it these fundamental changes in the nature and control of private property in America.

It also meant sweeping alterations in the spatial or geographical scale on which businesses operated. In simpler times before large-scale enterprises, many firms operated in a single town or city, often from a single office, store, or factory. Almost all manufacturing companies sold their goods in two ways. Some sales went to customers in the immediate area, and the rest of the product was sold through merchants in a nearby major city. For example, Baltimore iron merchant Enoch Pratt (through whose civic-minded generosity that city's public library system was later founded) sold the goods made by numerous manufacturers in Maryland, West Virginia, and Pennsylvania on the eve of the Civil War. The typical manufacturer had a very limited horizon, often living in ignorance of events and people in distant parts of the nation. Retailers exhibited a similar insularity. There were, of course, some in the business world whose work did require a knowledge of affairs over a broader area; merchants who dealt in international trade had existed since the Middle Ages, and in the American context, bankers and merchants acted as the connecting and coordinating units in the economy. Such mercantile actors had to play on a wide geographic stage, extending credit, making collections, buying, and selling. The banking house of Alexander Brown and Sons, analyzed in Edwin J. Perkins's *Financing Anglo-American Trade: The House of Brown, 1800–1880* (1975), assisted commercial transactions all over the world from their branches in New York, Baltimore, Liverpool, London, and other cities. Beginning in the colonial years and in the first few decades after the conclusion of the Revolutionary War, the general merchants of the seaboard cities, such as South Carolina's Henry Laurens, dealt with customers and suppliers all over the world. Despite that, their enterprises were not big businesses, but were instead very successful small ones, usually involving only a handful of people. Very few manufacturers, retailers, or others had substantial contacts outside the immediate area in which they did business.

This situation was overturned completely by the rise of big business. The giant enterprise of the turn of the century carried out its functions in a great many different, widely scattered locations. The old pattern of a single factory or distribution outlet per firm often gave way to one firm's having an array of production and/or distribution facilities. As they expanded their activities, railroads, manufacturing firms, and some retailers found their names becoming household words (often preceded by barroom adjectives) in states all over the union. The railroads laid their tracks and ran their trains over long distances, with single roads or systems eventually covering hundreds or thousands of miles and many states. Manufacturing corporations came to have numerous plants for the production of their goods, and later when individual firms diversified into various product lines, the number and kinds of factories, mills, and refineries per firm were still further increased. As manufacturing corporations took over some of the functions that had earlier belonged to independent businesses (functions such as wholesaling, transporting, and sometimes retailing), they operated in more and more widely scattered locales. For example, by 1900 General Electric had numerous plants in various locations and sales offices in twenty-three cities across the United States. By the early years of the twentieth century, as Mira Wilkins has chronicled in several comprehensive studies, a number of large American corporations had extended their business activities around the world. Leading European firms were forging multinational enterprises during the same years, and "those of Britain, Germany, France, and some of the smaller nations of western Europe began to invest in the United States, first in marketing establishments, then in factories and mines," as Alfred Chandler noted in his introduction to Wilkins's *History of Foreign Investment in the United States to 1914* (1989). Muckraking cartoons around the turn of the century often depicted the leading business giants of the day as spiders whose webs enveloped vast areas, ever ready to trap the unwary or the helpless. As the cartoons indicated, this new spatial dimension of business was deeply disturbing to Americans accustomed to the older order of local, small, single-site enterprises. Big business, like the Deity many citizens addressed on Sundays, seemed to be everywhere.

Not only did the coming of big business mean that private economic enterprises carried out their functions on a much wider geographic landscape, but it also meant that they engaged in many more kinds of business operations than had earlier firms. Although the great colonial seaport merchants had handled a wide range of activities in the early economy, many were supplanted by a new kind of business after 1815, when mercantile operations became more highly specialized. Most merchants tended to become primarily a wholesaler or retailer, an exporter or an importer, to have one particular kind of mercantile focus rather than a mixture of several. Furthermore, wholesalers often specialized in a single line of goods such as drugs, dry goods, hardware, or other articles. "By 1860," George Rogers Taylor wrote in *The Transportation Revolution, 1815–1860* (1951), "the organization of both foreign and domestic trade had reached a high degree of specialization."

Specialization had been even more characteristic of manufacturing operations. Manufacturers, whether small artisans or the owners of early factories, were usually specialized in function and in product. They were customarily producers only and they ordinarily made a single kind of item or a small number of similar goods. For example, an iron furnace of the 1850s normally made only pig (cast) iron; it did not convert the cast iron into semifinished wrought iron or into finished products such as nails or hardware. Separate businesses handled the processing of the cast iron—businesses such as forges, slitting mills, and rolling mills, none of which had any direct connection with the furnace. But in a big business such as Carnegie Steel in 1900, one firm made cast iron and steel plus a variety of other metal goods in its own rolling mills and forges. When mid-nineteenth-century manufacturers needed to market their products, they had turned to specialized wholesalers who handled the task of merchandising the goods to distant retailers or other customers. When producers needed to have goods transported, they had called on forwarding merchants or on the early traffic departments of railroads. For example, the ironmasters of 1850 would simply turn over the marketing of their cast iron to separate businesses (such as the one led by Baltimore iron merchant Enoch Pratt), which sold the goods and charged the ironmasters for the services rendered. Carnegie Steel, on the other hand, had its own company sales force by 1900. Similarly, in the business of raising, butchering, transporting, and selling fresh meat, each step in 1850 had been handled by a different, separate business. By 1900 firms such as Swift and Armour were doing the slaughtering, transporting, warehousing, and retailing of beef, all as a part of the same company's operations. The economic system of the United States in the mid-nineteenth century had been highly subdivided, and each business performed its special task with relatively little knowledge of related activities.

Many of the large manufacturing corporations altered that earlier system by expanding the range of a firm's functions and its products. Big businesses often combined under a single corporate roof the activities of obtaining raw materials, turning them into manufactured products, wholesaling the goods, and sometimes retailing them, as Glenn Porter and Harold C. Livesay demonstrated by examining a number of major corporations in *Merchants and Manufacturers* (1971). Many corporations also came to have their own internal traffic departments that handled the transportation of goods, sometimes via the companies' own fleets of trucks, ships, or railroad cars (Swift & Co. and Standard Oil are two such examples). And many large businesses were able to achieve a high degree of autonomy in the financial sphere as well, paying for improvements or new operations out of earlier earnings retained by the corporations, or issuing stocks or bonds whose acceptance rested more on the strength of the businesses than on the reputation of the bankers who underwrote the issues. In 1850 such financial independence was rare. An ironmaster or meatpacker had to rely for loans on separate businesses such as banks or big wholesalers. Antebellum merchants often loaned substantial amounts to manufacturers, and some merchants eventually transferred their skills into the field of banking, as illustrated by Elva Tooker's study of a Philadelphia metal merchant, *Nathan Trotter* (1955). By 1900, however, firms like Carnegie Steel and Armour & Co. were strong enough to enjoy a significant degree of independence from such outside financial sources.

The coming of big business saw an accumulation of various different economic functions within a single company (often called vertical integration), and unification made business units much more powerful and more fully the masters of their own economic fate. The leaders of giant firms found themselves freer to act and better able to control the course of their enterprises with "everything being within ourselves," as Andrew Carnegie once phrased it. As they multiplied their functions, so too did large-scale enterprises increase their range of products. Many of the new businesses abandoned the traditional pattern of narrow specialization and turned to the production of several different kinds of goods, especially as the twentieth century progressed. Some of the largest, most complex, and successful businesses in America and in Western Europe had learned before World War I to apply their talents and production facilities to a diversity of products within a single firm.

The proliferation of factories, the geographical spread of firms, the increasing variety of products, and most especially the integration of different areas of business within one enterprise necessitated a complete change in the way businesses were managed. In the days before giant enterprises, businesses required very little in the way of administrative networks. Mercantile, commercial, and financial enterprises usually involved only a few partners and a handful of (male) clerks who had a knowledge of bookkeeping and could write in the flowing, clear, formal business penmanship so useful in avoiding misunderstandings in the age before the typewriter and the word processor. The small manufacturing shops, peopled by an artisan-entrepreneur and a few workers or apprentices, likewise required little in the way of administration. Even the factories that arose before the Civil War involved only a manager, a few foremen, and a group of workers who normally all labored in the same building. Under such circumstances, it was relatively easy for owners or managers to oversee personally almost all the operations of their businesses. When something went wrong or could be improved, the bosses had only to shout out their wishes to the few workers toiling at the mill or the office. Similarly, because businesses seldom operated in more than one location, there were almost no problems of controlling distant operations. The only figures in business who normally engaged in activities in widely separated areas were the large merchants and bankers, and they tried to ensure accountability and honesty in distant branches by staffing them with relatives. Few concerns, however, had any such problems with the oversight of the firm or factory; those sorts of administrative challenges rarely arose before the advent of large-scale corporations.

As big businesses appeared in the American economy, however, they brought with them new administrative problems and the need for new managerial patterns. How could owners or managers know what was going on in the various locales? How could they make their decisions known to distant employees and see that they were effectively carried out? As the number of different kinds of functions performed by a single firm increased, the difficulties grew even more complex. How could the needs and capacities of the various divisions of the firm be ascertained and coordinated? How could the purchasing department supply the right amount and kinds of raw materials in the right sequence to ensure that factories or mills functioned efficiently? How could the marketing activities be geared to the rate of production to ensure a rational flow of goods into the market and thus minimize fluctuations in prices and profits? The success of the venture depended on a great many separate but interrelated activities, all of which had to be managed well to see that the internal rhythm of the enterprise was intelligently controlled and coordinated. Everything was contingent on something else, and it was all scattered about the landscape. No one individual could possibly oversee the operation personally.

The solutions to the new and perplexing problems of management could be found only through the creation of elaborate, formal administrative networks, the bureaucracies that are the characteristic organizational form of institutions in the modern world. To work efficiently, business had to be carefully organized, with various levels of managers making and implementing both the long-range planning for the venture as a whole and the day-to-day operations of its far-flung divisions. Formal, written rules were created to govern affairs ranging from the selection of qualified personnel to the operation of the production and distribution processes to the procedures for firing top managers and clerks. Clear lines of authority and control had to be devised so that people understood their roles, responsibilities, authority, and accountability. Only by building such an elaborate administrative network was it possible for big business to avoid chaos. For the first time, businesses required middle managers as well as those at the top and on the bottom of organizations.

A major challenge was devising systems and technologies for handling the enormous volume of information generated within a modern firm. Intelligent management requires accurate, comprehensible, retrievable data, in vast quantities. As JoAnne Yates's *Control through Communication: The Rise of System in American Management* (1989) demonstrated by examining the history of Du Pont, the Illinois Central Railroad, and the Scoville Manufacturing Company, it was not easy to work out the means through which information and communications could flow down, up, and laterally throughout a complex business. The storage, summary, and retrieval of massive amounts of data presented a thorny problem for a business system accustomed to keeping its meager records in a few handwritten volumes and boxes of correspondence. Generations of new typing and copying devices began to evolve, along with new filing and storage systems, to satisfy the organization's voracious requirements for information and communications. With big business began a communications revolution that would in time produce the computer and the development of the "information society."

When business innovators began to create large-scale enterprises in the last half of the nineteenth century, they were usually unaware of these administrative problems. Often the results were chaotic. Rather than reaping the benefits of expanded and dispersed operations, they sometimes found themselves encountering losses because of their inability to solve complex managerial problems. The transition to big business was often a confused, experimental process that produced more failures than successes. Many prominent railroads had gone bankrupt and been reorganized several times by the 1890s, and many of the early combinations in manufacturing were complete failures. Because the institution of big business was new, those who built large corporations had to feel their way through the early years. Because they were trying something novel, they had very few sources of informed and experienced assistance. Only after businesses had arisen whose size and complexity called for correspondingly large and dense bureaucratic managerial structures did universities create graduate management schools in the first decade of the twentieth century to train people to run big businesses. Management became a very different and considerably more difficult job after the rise of large-scale business concerns, and the prospect of a single manager running such a venture efficiently disappeared.

As large corporations began to build the elaborate bureaucracies necessary for their existence, another profound difference between the mid nineteenth-century concern and the turn-of-the-century giant enterprise emerged—business began to lose its highly personal tone. Almost from the earliest days of economic endeavors among the European colonists, businesses were extensions of the personalities of those who ran them. The way in which businesses dealt with other businesses—with assurance and respect or with misgivings and extreme caution—depended on the personal character and wealth of individuals. In large part, this was because very few concerns were widely owned or were organized in corporate form. A business was worth only as much as its owners and their partners, and business success rested heavily on how others perceived one's character. Because almost the entire early economy functioned on credit (few were able to pay cash, and payment after six, twelve, or eighteen months was common), the confidence of creditors in an individual often determined the ability of that person's business to expand during good times or to survive in bad times. The whole ethos of nineteenth-century individualism and what today seems small-town morality was closely related to these interwoven values and attitudes toward business. When Lewis Tappan founded his Mercantile Agency in the 1840s (the first nationwide credit bureau and a forerunner of Dun and Bradstreet), the credit rating of a business was influenced almost as much by the character and personal habits of its owners as by the profits of the firm. The good owner-entrepreneur was sober, honest, diligent, hardworking, and shrewd—an amalgam of the old puritan virtues harnessed in pursuit of profit. Such people did not hang around saloons or associate with unsavory characters—or at least they did so only with the same discretion and shrewdness they brought to their leatherbound journals and day books. Firms were merely the cloaks that individuals put on to do business; as an antebellum phrase put it, a firm's name was simply the current "style" of those running the enterprise. Perhaps the clearest indication of the personal tone of business was the fact that it was common for a firm to die along with its owner.

Relationships between owner-managers and their workers were also quite personal. Because the managers saw their few employees frequently and lived with them in the same town, the bosses could at least be expected to know their workers' names, the quality of their work, and perhaps even some things about their personal lives. Large organizations, however, required layers of management, complex personnel functions to handle "human relations," and, in unionized firms, elaborate work rules and formal grievance procedures. The nature of relationships between the labor force and the managers, as well as the highly individual identification of persons with their firms, underwent considerable change in big business by 1920.

A necessary concomitant of bureaucracy was impersonality; a complex administrative network created a social and economic gap between those on various levels of the hierarchy. As the operations of a single business grew larger, more involved, and more widely separated, employees often had no knowledge of the distant, almost disembodied people who controlled and manipulated the business and thus affected their lives so strongly. As more and more technologically advanced production processes appeared, work became highly mechanized and routinized. Management came to exercise increasing control over shop-floor conditions that previously had been labor's domain. Work itself, as well as one's relations with others in the organization, grew more impersonal.

This impersonality spread to the owners and managers as well. As ownership was diffused among many people via incorporation and public purchase of stock, businesses began to lose their aura of identification with a single owner or with several partners. Corporations became potentially immortal institutions whose owners were numerous, changing, and not easily identified. As professional managers with little ownership rose to positions of power in the corporate world, many firms assumed an air of anonymity and facelessness. The importance of character and individual reliability in business dealings diminished as a company assumed a life of its own apart from that of the persons who staffed and served it. As anyone who has ever dealt with a modern bureaucracy understands, one could no longer simply go in and settle a dispute or misunderstanding by exchanging some straight talk with the owner. The locus of power and responsibility often seemed as elusive as the Cheshire cat in Wonderland, despite (and, paradoxically, also because of) the elaborate rules, the standardized procedures, and the supposedly clear lines of authority and control.

The years of the rise of big business hardly represented an unambiguous picture of the shift from a highly personal to a very impersonal business world. As is always the case, events do not conform easily to the generalizations historians offer to try to make sense of the past. Although the years 1860–1920 did mark the rise of the giant, impersonal corporation, they also seem in many ways to be the most highly personalized era in the entire history of American business. During the transitional period between the origin of firms that became large, complex enterprises and the subsequent triumph of diffused ownership and professional management, there emerged that fascinating generation so intimately associated in the public mind with the coming of big business. The era of the "trusts" was conceptualized by Americans of the time (and by many later historians) in terms of the business leaders who symbolized the early giant corporations—magnates like John D. Rockefeller, Gustavus Swift, Philip Armour, James B. Duke, Henry Havemeyer, Andrew Carnegie, William Vanderbilt, and the most influential of them all, John Pierpont Morgan.

It is not hard to understand why it seemed an age of business titans, robber barons, and industrial giants. First, there was considerable justification for thinking of the corporations in terms of the founders, at least for a time. They usually held a large chunk of ownership, if not a controlling interest, and many of them did at first play decisive managerial roles in their enterprises. Furthermore, it seems to be almost a universal human trait to adopt the mental shorthand of identifying, if possible, a single person with the larger entity, especially if that entity is thought to be evil: Hitler symbolized the whole of Nazi Germany, the Bank of the United States was "Biddle's Bank," and so on. The large railroads and the pioneering manufacturing corporations such as Standard Oil, American Sugar, American Tobacco, and others seemed even larger than life and more awesomely powerful than they actually were, simply because they were the first such institutions Americans had seen. They were novel and unfamiliar, and the people who symbolized them seemed all the more mysteriously grand and ominously impressive as a result.

Of course, in no case did any of the legendary business giants really control directly many of the numerous and varied activities of the enterprises associated with their names. It was impossible for those at the top to penetrate very far into complex bureaucracies; such operations depended on many people. And those who provided the initial innovative idea or the leadership to launch a big business often found their degree of ownership and control diminishing as the firms grew. James B. Duke, for example, learned that he had to share control of American Tobacco with outside bankers and financiers well before the government's successful antitrust suit was completed in 1911. After a national market for industrial securities arose in the 1890s, and as management increasingly became the province of skilled, salaried professionals, even the public vision of big business leaders began to blur. (Growing anonymity may have been a factor in the decline in public criticism of big business after the mid-1890s, as documented in Louis Galambos, *The Public Image of Big Business in America, 1880–1940,* 1975.) In reality, the generation of giants (the lords of creation, Frederick Lewis Allen called some of them) acted as midwives in the birth of the modern corporation. Their achievements were great, their talents considerable, and their fortunes enormous. But if they had not called forth the new institution of large-scale business enterprise, others would probably have done so, for its time had clearly come. In this sense, their personal stamp on the era is somewhat illusory, for the businesses they began quickly outgrew their ability to control or manage them. The impersonal, institutional demands of giant firms shaped new patterns of ownership and management by the opening years of the twentieth century, eclipsing the brief but exceedingly bright glow of the generation whose names had for a time symbolized big business.

Whether the giant corporations were personal or impersonal, a final aspect of big business that should be emphasized is that they represented very great conglomerations of wealth and power. Although the business world before 1850 produced some extremely rich individuals and some influential companies, it had nothing comparable to the accumulated wealth and power embodied in the huge firms of the late nineteenth and early twentieth centuries. Decisions made by the managers of giant enterprises touched the lives of thousands and could affect the course of the wider economy. A whole new middle class of managers arose with the corporation, and their values and influence soon supplanted those of the earlier professional, mercantile, and agrarian elites throughout American society. A few people became rich on a scale never before possible, and they naturally wielded the power that accompanies such wealth in the United States. Although it is difficult to judge whether the influence of business as a whole in American life was increased (it had always been great), there is little doubt that the rise of big business meant the heightened concentration of economic and social power in the hands of a very few. Fear of that power and its relative distance from the democratic process contributed mightily to the misgivings that Americans felt about the huge new economic institutions that arose in their society.

The most important, defining characteristic of those institutions lay in the fact that they represented a new kind of highly productive economic organism, structurally and functionally different from the ones that had occupied the landscape previously. A large-scale corporate enterprise, as we have seen, differed substantially from earlier businesses in a number of respects: its capital requirements; its cost structure; its market power; the nature of its ownership; the geographic scale on which it operated; its performance of a variety of economic functions embodied in a range of goods and services; its managerial and administrative requirements; its anonymity and impersonality; and its great wealth, power, and influence in American society. These attributes were the hallmarks of the giant business concerns, characteristics that explain what big business was, how it worked, and how it represented a new institution in the United States and indeed in the world.

The coming of these new economic institutions had fundamental and far-reaching implications for American society. The effects on our political history were immediate; much of the bitter conflict associated with populism, progressivism, and the New Deal resulted from the rise and spread of big businesses and disagreements over the proper role of such organizations in American life. The appearance of giant firms compelled a troubling, difficult examination of the nation's deepest political values. As we will see, it forced Americans to measure their traditional fear of concentrated private economic power against their fear of concentrated power in the form of economic planning by the state. The result ultimately proved to be compromise in the form of a regulated, rather than a planned, economy.

The advent of giant, bureaucratically administered, highly productive corporations brought for most Americans changes in the nature of work, in the communities in which they made their homes and secured their livelihoods, in the level of their consumption of material goods, in their values, and in the quality of their lives. Americans cast off their older roles as producers and embraced a new consumer culture. Modern advertising emerged as a leading engine of the new, corporate, consumer world by the early twentieth century. As Jackson Lears wrote in *Fables of Abundance* (1994), "advertising collaborated with other institutions in promoting what became the dominant aspirations, anxieties, even notions of personal identity, in the modern United States." The society remade itself to accommodate to the needs of the modern corporation. A new technical, bureaucratic middle class arose whose values and culture came to dominate and define life in the United States, which Olivier Zunz analyzed in *Making America Corporate, 1870–1920,* (1990). People left the country and moved to the city, despite all the changes that caused in their daily lives, to get what they saw as benefits from the new patterns of working and living. If, as Richard Hofstadter once suggested, the most important fact about this nation's history is that it grew up in the country and moved to the city, it is vital to recall why the move was made. Americans embraced the new industrial, corporate order primarily because they saw it as a more promising environment in terms of their material well-being and the possibilities for economic and social progress for themselves and their families. In time they also came to accept it because there seemed to be no real alternative, no way of turning back the clock without abandoning the market system and limited government.

These developments in the United States were merely the first wave in what would in time become almost a worldwide phenomenon. The United States led the way in the creation of a corporate, market-driven civilization, but other nations followed, some very soon and others at a later time. National patterns certainly differed significantly in timing and in the various ways in which the modern corporation appeared. (This can be seen in such studies as Mansel G. Blackford's *The Rise of Modern Business in Great Britain, the United States, and Japan,* 1988.) America's economic, social, and political system provided an especially fertile soil in which the new, technologically advanced, complex, and bureaucratically administered business organization flourished. It drew on traditions, values, and attitudes rooted in the distant past as it shaped new ones. Though its triumph was contested and never entirely complete, it proved to be a revolutionary institution.

Much good as well as much that was not good has flowed from the emergence of our corporate, technologically advanced, urban (and now suburban) nation. Whatever one's view of the ultimate worth or shortcomings of the particular kind of world we have built, it is clear that the modern corporation lies at the heart of it. Until we understand how and why we came to have that particular institution, we cannot fully understand our society nor intelligently judge the desirability and the possibility of change.

CHAPTER TWO

The Appearance and Spread of Big Business

The Advent of Industrialization

When General Pierre Gustave Toutant Beauregard ordered the shelling of Fort Sumter in Charleston's harbor in the spring of 1861, there was only one sector in the economy that included firms that could legitimately be called big businesses in the sense in which the term was used in the preceding chapter. That was the railroads, and at that point in our national history, they were still widely regarded as an almost unalloyed good. By the time of the Supreme Court's dissolution of Standard Oil, American Tobacco, and Du Pont a half-century later, such firms dominated much of the center of the American economy. They came slowly at first, appearing here and there in manufacturing by the 1880s, adding to the concerns that produced the Sherman Antitrust Act in 1890. The pace then quickened, and they came in a torrent in the last years of the nineteenth and the first years of the twentieth century.

We often think of industrialization and factories in conjunction with the rise of big business, but in fact the appearance of the factory did not at first call forth giant enterprises. Although industrialization certainly had its greatest impact in the age of big business, it had begun before mammoth enterprises appeared in manufacturing, and it continued in many medium and small firms after the spread of the large corporation. Both Western Europe and the United States had moved decisively into the era of the industrial revolution before the appearance of giant, bureaucratically administered firms. Beginning late in the eighteenth century, new technologies of production, novel machines, and the classic combination of steam, coal, and iron had given the world powerful ways of increasing the supply of goods. Britain led the way, with the young United States quickly joining in the exploration along what Thomas C. Cochran called economic and social *Frontiers of Change* (1979). And at least as early as the time of the War of 1812, the American textile industry operated what one could call true factories. Francis Cabot Lowell founded the Boston Manufacturing Company in 1813, and that firm created in Waltham, Massachusetts, the nation's first textile mill combining weaving and spinning operations within a single factory. Caroline F. Ware's classic book *Early New England Cotton Manufacture* (1931) documented the spread of similar "Lowell Mills" throughout other parts of New England where water power was available. In the initial decades after the passage of the Constitution, early factories appeared in many other industries as well. Along the lovely Brandywine River in Delaware there arose a cluster of early factories, including the water-powered gunpowder mills of what would one day become become one of the largest corporations in the nation, Du Pont. New York City and Philadelphia (including their environs) became great centers of manufacturing in the young republic. Throughout the Northeast, particularly along the "fall line," where the drop of rivers and streams approaching the Atlantic provided water power, industrialization had its beginnings in America.

By the 1840s the factory came to many industries. Although American producers were slow to adopt both steam technology and the advances in ironmaking underway in Britain by the

1830s, the 1840s and 1850s saw the spread of steam power and great progress in the American metalworking industries. As steam became available as a source of power for manufacturing, businesses could locate factories in new places, even sites that did not enjoy access to water power. This made it much easier for producers to operate near or in any urban center that offered a labor force or a potentially large market. Similarly, manufacturers could choose sites closer to raw material sources if they wished. In industries such as the manufacture of firearms, clocks, and nails, Americans led the world into new methods of mass production using specialized machines, a set of arrangements that later came to be known as "the American system" of manufactures. At the London Crystal Palace Exhibition in 1851, the world's manufacturers displayed the best of their goods and machines, and the American displays attracted great attention and admiration. As Brooke Hindle and Steven Lubar indicated in their *Engines of Change* (1987), the American triumph at that first of the great international world's fairs symbolized the industrial maturity of the United States on the global stage. By the close of the 1850s, then, the American economy was well launched into industrialization and rapid, sustained growth. A strong increase in the demand for goods arose within the developing regional hinterlands as the population spread westward, and established manufacturing centers such as Philadelphia grew rapidly, as shown in Diane Lindstrom's *Economic Development in the Philadelphia Region, 1810–1850* (1978). The economy now grew at a rate consistently higher than in previous eras of history. While scholars have argued for many years about the timing and sources of the transition to faster, sustained economic growth, most would agree that the United States was well on the road to industrialization and virtually continuous, long-term economic growth by 1860.

The national march toward mechanized production and the spread of factories did not, however, immediately trigger the appearance of big business in manufacturing. For many years thereafter, business continued to be done in single-plant operations, ownership of individual units was still concentrated among small numbers of people, ownership and management still customarily went hand in hand, manufacturers generally specialized in a single product or a single line of goods, and industry was not yet the province of complex, bureaucratically administered networks. In regional markets, firms still competed mostly based on price. Many small firms, however, flourished because they operated in island communities where, as Stanley L. Engerman and Kenneth L. Sokoloff pointed out in the *Cambridge Economic History of the United States* (2000), "high transport costs provided local monopolies," and consumers had to pay higher prices as a result. On the eve of the Civil War the economy remained dominated by merchants. Almost all citizens shared a belief in the desirability of material growth, and the most rancorous political controversies over the power of big businesses still lay in the future. Of all the economic institutions on the American scene in 1860, only the railroads qualified as big businesses, and their greatest time of political trouble still lay ahead.

Pioneers in Big Business: The Railroads

Railroads brought new methods of management, new forms of corporate finance, different dimensions in labor relations, new ways of competition, and a new relationship between business and government. They also created the first modern corporate bureaucracies and recruited and trained the first generation of a new managerial middle class. In his *The Railroads, the Nation's First Big Business* (1965) and in many of his subsequent writings, Alfred Chandler made a strong case for the pathbreaking role of railroads in meeting and resolving many of the problems later faced by other giant enterprises.

In the financial sphere, the railroads presented problems on a scale never faced before in the United States, and they called forth innovative responses. During their construction in the 1830s, railroads, then a wholly new form of transportation, had relied on heavy financial aid from state governments (as had many canals earlier in the century). The depression of the late 1830s and early 1840s, however, severely affected the states' purses and credit ratings, and the great railroad expansion of the 1850s had to proceed with less government assistance. The growth of the railroads in that decade put unprecedented strains on the economy's ability to mobilize capital. In the ten years after 1850, the nation's railroad mileage more than tripled, going from 9,000 to more than 30,000 miles. By the end of that decade, as Henry Varnum Poor's *History of the Railroads and Canals of the United States of America* (1860) showed, numerous companies had capital accounts of more than $10 million. Several, including the east-west trunk lines such as the New York Central, the Baltimore & Ohio (B&O), and the New York and Erie, were valued at more than $20 million. Most of the money to finance the growth of the rail system came from private investors, though some support came from the federal government and states, cities, and counties eager to encourage the expansion of their transportation networks. Never before in the history of the nation had such funds been required for economic ventures; even the most expensive canal, New York's Erie, had cost only about $7 million. The result of this new demand for capital was that America's money and investment markets were centralized where they have remained since—on Wall Street. The stocks and bonds of railroads all over the nation began to be listed and actively traded on the New York Stock Exchange as the resources of investors in the United States and Europe were mobilized in support of railways. At the same time, the modern investment-banking house appeared in order to handle the marketing of this abundance of new securities. Perhaps the earliest firm to provide the services now associated with investment banking, Winslow, Lanier & Co., began in New York in 1849 and flourished on the negotiation of railroad securities, as explained in Vincent Carosso's *Investment Banking in America, A History* (1970). In the 1850s, Carosso noted, such companies "contributed substantially toward making New York City the principal center of American railroad finance." As we will see later, a similar revolution in the nation's capital markets in the 1890s permitted and encouraged the flood of large industrial combinations around the turn of the century. The railroads, however, were the first businesses to require such large amounts of capital that they marshaled savings of people from all over America and abroad.

The complexity of the railroads' operations also brought new managerial as well as financial difficulties. "Railroad managers," wrote JoAnne Yates in *Control through Communication* (1989), "were pioneers in managerial theory and practice. They anticipated the systematic management philosophy in arguing for the need to systematize procedures independent of the individuals involved and to use systematically gathered operational information as the basis for evaluation and decision making at higher levels." A large railroad's activities extended over hundreds of miles and involved enormous problems of planning, coordination, and control. The number of financial transactions handled by a road's conductors, station agents, and freight agents required a central controller's office, begun first by the B&O. The scheduling of the flow of equipment to match expected demand over the system also called for new managerial structures. The long- and short-term capital needs of the giant enterprises had to be carefully planned, and the railroads became the first businesses to achieve modern cost analysis or cost accounting to anticipate financial demands and measure the firm's performance, including comparisons between divisions, managers, and workers. These and other problems, on both a day-to-day and a long-term basis, called forth bureaucratically structured administrative networks to manage the voluminous, complex activities of the railways.

No manufacturing companies faced such difficulties until later in the nineteenth century. When they did arise in other industries, many firms turned to the management experience of the railroads as a guide. Indeed, the railways proved a fertile training ground for those who later ran big businesses in the manufacturing sector. Andrew Carnegie was probably the most famous "graduate" of the nation's premier railroad, the Pennsylvania, to go on to oversee another large-scale enterprise, but rail managers moved into many other kinds of companies because they knew how to run complicated, diverse, widely dispersed enterprises. The same was also true in other nations as well. When big business spread through much of Britain's economy after World War I, persons skilled in the complex challenges of operating the railways there were much in demand in other sectors of the economy. And when graduate schools of business administration appeared in the United States shortly after the turn of the century, the managerial principles derived from the experience of the railroads played an important role in their courses.

In some ways, the railroads were also leaders in forging new patterns of labor relations. Their workers were among the first to operate in an impersonal, bureaucratically controlled environment, and they were among the first to achieve collective bargaining and grievance channels through their national unions, the railroad brotherhoods. Initially these unions, like many other early American labor organizations, were social and mutual benefit societies. By the 1870s, though, they were evolving into modern unions. Like many of the craft unions that formed the American Federation of Labor (AFL) in the 1880s, the railway brotherhoods derived their negotiating strength from the fact that their members had specialized and hard-to-replace skills. A strike by such a union was a real threat to employers because it was extremely difficult to break the strike by bringing in outside workers ("scabs" in union parlance). Furthermore, the railway workers were empowered by the fact that they controlled the use and maintenance of expensive equipment. The unhappy history of unions that tried to include a broad range of the nation's working people, such as the National Labor Union and the Knights of Labor, indicated that it was very difficult, if not impossible, to create and sustain unions unless the members had specialized skills like the railroad workers and the members of the craft unions that joined together to form the AFL.

The giant corporations that arose in manufacturing, however, proved to be much more successful in fighting off unionization than were the railways. Most of the new big businesses came in industries that relied on semiskilled rather than skilled workers, and unions found it extremely difficult to make headway, a problem exacerbated by the hostile legal and political environment for unions in America. Not until the New Deal, when the Wagner Act (1935) gave legal status to democratically chosen collective bargaining units (unions) and brought the power of the federal government to bear on employers, were industrial big businesses participants in the kind of labor relations found on the railroads in the late nineteenth century.

The railroads were also the first businesses to encounter competitive problems flowing from the fact that they did not fit the classical conception of many small competitors being guided by the invisible hand of the market, as portrayed by eighteenth-century economist Adam Smith. In part this was due to their status as "natural monopolies." Once society had made the great investment necessary to build and operate a railroad between two given points, it was much less useful to add additional routes between those same two points. As the nation's railroad network proliferated, however, it became increasingly common to see just such competing routes. Often the only meaningful competitive weapon such railroads had against each other was the price of the transport services they offered. This encouraged price wars, as different roads fought for the opportunity to carry the limited passengers and freight. This problem was worsened by the perception among railroaders that they already had such great fixed costs sunk in their systems that it cost them almost nothing to carry an additional car or two on any given train. They were therefore encouraged to cut prices, offer rebates, and hand out free passes liberally in order to persuade passengers and shippers to use their line rather than that of a competitor. Almost any revenue, they thought, was a net gain, since they were running the trains anyway and their variable costs were negligible. As the work of Gregory Thompson has shown, this belief that the railroads had hardly any variable costs was wrong, but it became an article of faith in the industry, persisting for many decades and powerfully influencing managerial behavior. Since railroad leaders believed strongly in the notion of fixed costs, the idea exacerbated the price wars already underway as a result of the railroads' status as natural monopolies. The result was that the railroad sector came to have a constantly changing crazy-quilt system of rates. The chaos alienated the public, and the managers of this vital sector experienced grave economic problems.

Such a situation could be alleviated only by some kind of formal cooperation between railroad companies or by the creation of a central body to set and enforce consistent, reasonably fair rates in an effort to satisfy both the railroaders and the public interest. The unhappy state of affairs, in other words, could be relieved only by cooperation among the competitors.

The railroads attempted for a long time to bring order in their own house by joining together to create an American variant of the European cartel (usually called *pools* or *associations* here) in an attempt to fix rates or allocate traffic between cooperating roads. This represented an effort to retain a strong degree of independence among the "competing" businesses, yet safeguard profits for the cooperating firms through private regulation of rates and traffic. The roads tried many types of pools and associations, some of which included provisions for fines for members who violated the rates or sought traffic outside the approved channels of the association. Later there emerged other cooperative efforts called "communities of interest," in which the roads bought stock in each other and placed representatives on each other's boards of directors. All these ingenious efforts were aimed at the paradoxical end of ensuring "fair competition" by blunting or avoiding competition. All were indications that, from the point of view of the railroads, the market mechanism was not working very well in their industry.

Although they sometimes enjoyed brief periods of success, almost all such efforts to control competition in the railroad industry eventually failed. That outcome was in part the result of the natural economics of the transportation sector, but it also had much to do with the fact that the persons overseeing such cooperative undertakings as the pools could not enforce their agreements through the legal system. At first the arrangements were not actually illegal, but they lacked the force of contracts, which the courts did of course enforce. In Great Britain and on the Continent, the legal systems were much more sympathetic to cartels, though the mere fact that a cartel's agreement was legally enforceable was no guarantee that competition could be controlled or profits assured. In the United States all such arrangements were voluntary and thus could not be enforced by law, and competitive pressures usually made it impossible to prevent one of the cooperating companies from breaking its promises by cutting rates or hogging traffic in an effort to better its own position. Rate breaking often was done in secret, through rebates in which a railroad returned a part of its charges to shippers in order to get their business. In addition, of course, railroad pools and associations raised very serious political questions about the fairness and legality of businesses conspiring to set rates through collaboration among theoretically competing firms. The fact that some shippers received unequal treatment from the railroads and thus had to compete under the heavy burden of higher transportation rates made the question of fairness even more urgent.

The political response was not long in coming. The railroads became the first major industry after the Civil War to be the target of widespread political attacks. Mercantile and shipping interests combined with agrarian groups to provide the impetus for the passage of a series of state laws in the 1870s that came to be called the Granger laws, after the farm cooperative organization that supported them. The purpose of that legislation was to set maximum rates and outlaw the charging of higher rates for short hauls than for long ones. In fact, from the standpoint of costs, it was usually more expensive per ton-mile for railroads to load, unload, and rearrange freight cars frequently for a group of short hauls than to route shipments on long hauls between two major rail points. As railroad historian Albro Martin wrote in *Enterprise Denied: Origins of the Decline of American Railroads, 1897–1917* (1971), "no rate-making practice was more firmly rooted in the economic realities of railroad competition." But this apparent discrimination nevertheless drew much public criticism. After the Supreme Court's

1886 *Wabash, St. Louis & Pacific Railroad Company* v. *Illinois* case ruling that only Congress could regulate interstate commerce, the state regulations aimed at remedying situations such as this were severely weakened. Pressure grew for national legislation to outlaw pooling and to prohibit rate discrimination.

Additional public concern over the railroads had its origins in the unsavory financial wheeling and dealing of such railroad promoters as Jay Gould and Jim Fisk. Manipulating the prices of securities through what we would now call "insider trading," bribing legislators and judges to gain a competitive advantage, and bilking unwary speculators intent on easy money, such buccaneers weakened some railroads and virtually destroyed others. These escapades inspired an early, delightful contribution to the robber baron view of the coming of big business, *Chapters of Erie* (1886) by Charles Francis Adams, Jr., and his brother Henry. "Pirates . . . are not extinct;" they lamented in a heavily punctuated passage, "they have only transferred their operations to the land, and conducted them in more or less accordance with the law; until, at last, so great a proficiency have they attained, that the commerce of the world is more equally but far more heavily taxed in their behalf, than would ever have entered into their wildest hopes while, outside the law, they simply made all comers stand and deliver." Congress responded to the cries for action in 1887 by passing the Interstate Commerce Act.

The federal government's regulatory role was weak for a time, but later legislation during the progressive era (including the Hepburn Act of 1906, the Mann-Elkins Act of 1910, and the Transportation Act of 1920) converted the railroads into a fully regulated industry whose rates were set by the Interstate Commerce Commission. Only some form of cartel could solve the peculiar competitive problems of the railways, and the eventual political solution turned out to be one big federally administered cartel.

Although it is easy to see the desirability of control by a regulatory body that would take into account both the interests of the railroad and the public, it is also clear that the regulatory job done by the Interstate Commerce Commission was not a particularly good one. Albro Martin, in his *Enterprise Denied*

(1971), for example, denounced the regulation spawned by "archaic Progressives," finding it so inept and harshly punitive that he blamed it for much of the later decline of the nation's railroads. Many other historians and also economists have been critical of the regulatory job done by the ICC; James W. Ely, Jr.'s *Railroads and American Law* (2001) was one of many studies that asserted that the regulators never truly understood the economics of the industry. Others would argue that the ICC was—like most regulatory commissions—dominated by the industry it was charged with regulating and thus never functioned effectively. Subsequent scholarship by Gregory L. Thompson, on the other hand, blamed poor management by the railroad leaders themselves for part of the industry's plight in the twentieth century. However one may choose to apportion the blame, it is clear that the difficulties of resolving the competitive dilemma presented by the railways were great and that the nation did not solve them very well. Most of that story, however, belongs to the period after World War I, when railroads were unable to compete with the automobile, the truck, and traffic on federally subsidized waterways. The railroads nevertheless were the first big businesses to grapple with the difficulties of competing in a setting where the normal market forces no longer worked very well. As a result, they pioneered new ways of competition among just a few firms. Big businesses in manufacturing industries, as we will see, encountered somewhat similar problems, but the difficulties they faced were not as acute as those of the railroads, and the solutions were somewhat different.

The railroads also led the way in another fashion in the history of American business, as demonstrated by Steven W. Usselman's pathbreaking study, *Regulating Railroad Innovation* (2002). Once the basic technological and commercial system of the railroads was in place, it became very costly and risky to introduce truly fundamental changes. The managers of such a complex system felt the need to control and channel change carefully. They therefore created a pattern of limited technological innovation. They wanted and did secure further improvements once they had built the basic system, and their productivity in fact improved markedly, but they clearly sought progress of a constrained sort. They were careful that new technologies and methods did not threaten or fundamentally disrupt the existing order, for that order embodied massive investments and countless settled arrangements. This policy made the railroads particularly vulnerable when fundamental changes arose *outside* their industry—when automobiles, trucks, and airplanes appeared in the twentieth century.

Attempts to regulate or constrain innovation in a controlled manner would characterize later big businesses based on science and technology—such as mainframe computers and silver nitrate-based photography. This preference for constrained, measured technical progress was vulnerable to criticism on the grounds that society as a whole suffered. Firms with market power and relatively tight short-term control over their industries could often be inflexible and resistant to progress. In this arena, as in so many others, the railroads set a pattern for giant businesses.

Preconditions for Big Business

In looking at the appearance and spread of big business in the manufacturing sector of the economy, it is important to keep in mind that there were two distinct periods within the general time-span covered in this book. The first period went up to about 1895, a time marked by the relatively slow, sporadic appearance of big business. The second witnessed the great explosion of mergers, from around 1895 to 1905. By about 1910, much of the industrial structure of the modern United States had been changed, and a great many of the giant corporations familiar to later Americans already were established as powerful economic institutions. We will focus initially on the period of slow growth prior to the great turn-of-the-century proliferation of large-scale enterprises.

Various conditions had to be met before the giant corporation could arise in American manufacturing, perhaps the most important of which was improved access to the commodity the railroads were created to supply—transportation. Nationally oriented firms were a product of a national market, and that did not exist until the United States had in place a comprehensive transportation network. Turning first to the early turnpikes, then to canals, and then to railroads, nineteenth-century Americans tied more and more of the nation together with increasingly reliable and more affordable ways of moving people and products. These improvements in transport and communications began the erosion of the island communities within the econ-omy and the society. With each step forward in this arena, Americans benefited, both socially and economically, from participation in larger and more specialized networks. First locales, then re-gions, and then the nation as a whole became more integrated and unified.

Much of the subsequent success of the national economy rested on the existence of a large domestic market, which made the fruits of industrialization available. That huge internal market relied on a well-developed transportation system. After the completion of New York's Erie Canal in 1825, numerous states followed in the construction of waterways designed to encourage economic expansion. Other cities and regions selected the newer means of transportation, the railroad. Cooperation between the business community of Baltimore and the state of Maryland, for example, resulted in that city's pathbreaking role in choosing a rail route (the B&O) rather than a canal to the interior. In a pro-cess described in encyclopedic detail in the *History of Transpor-tation in the United States before 1860* (prepared by Caroline E. MacGill and others under the direction of Balthasar Henry Meyer, 1917), the nation's avenues of transport grew ever-more numerous and lengthy. By the end of the 1850s, more than 3,000 miles of canals and 30,000 miles of railroads had been completed. Canal construction was on the wane by about 1850, but the rail network grew substantially until the close of the 1880s, totaling about 165,000 miles of road in operation in 1890. By the time of the explosive merger movement at the end of the century, in fact, the nation probably had more lines than it really needed because of duplication of facilities and expansion into some areas without enough traffic to support a railway.

The importance of this transportation system to the coming of big business was great. Only a national market could call forth truly large, nationally oriented manufacturing corporations. As long as the transportation system remained crude and incomplete, the costs of marketing goods in distant areas remained too high to encourage entry into those regions. Even if a manufacturer were an efficient producer, the high cost of carrying goods over considerable distances would add so much to the final price that the manufacturer could not compete with local sellers whose products need travel much shorter distances. For example, Norman L. Crockett's study of *The Woolen Industry of the Midwest* (1970) demonstrated that larger, more efficient eastern mills had no hope of breaking into the midwestern markets until shipping costs declined. "Transportation charges on eastern manufactures shipped to the Middle West declined steadily during the 1870s and 1880s," Crockett noted, "and in the process woolen mills in the region lost a substantial portion of their previous protection from eastern shippers." The railroads ended the protection enjoyed by many other regional industries throughout the rest of the nineteenth century. The construction of a good nationwide transport system was, therefore, a necessary economic precondition for the rise of big business, for only such a system could create a national market.

It was perhaps also necessary from a psychological point of view. Earlier in the century, a manufacturer was simply not likely to think of penetrating distant markets unreachable by water. Overland transport was prohibitively expensive, except for the lightest and most valuable goods. Only after the transportation revolution "shrank" the nation did Americans begin to dream of building far-flung manufacturing empires.

The second crucial development to the rise of big business was a revolution closely related to the vast changes in transportation—a communications revolution. As we saw earlier, the late-nineteenth- and early-twentieth-century giant enterprises engaged in many different kinds of highly interrelated functions over large geographic areas. This implied the ability to communicate rapidly and reliably, which the early-nineteenth-century businesses simply did not have. Communication by mail was very slow and uncertain. Businesses would, for example, often send several copies of the same letter or bill to improve the likelihood of getting the message delivered. Improvements and expansion in the postal system after 1790 were dramatic and improved business communication, as Richard R. John's *Spreading the News* (1995) showed. But the real breakthrough came with the telegraph.

In the two decades from 1846 through 1866, the telegraph industry grew from a primitive system with a few lines along the eastern seaboard to a comprehensive web of wires spanning the nation. Cementing an early, mutually beneficial partnership, the telegraph and the railroad marched together across the continent. Telegraph lines were built along railroad rights-of-way, thus saving the telegraph companies high land-clearing costs. The railroads, because they were complex, large-scale enterprises, found the telegraph essential to the intricate operations of their large rail systems. Moving steadily toward a private monopoly in those two decades, the telegraph industry emerged in 1866 as virtually a single firm, Western Union.

As the industry's leading historian, Robert L. Thompson, pointed out in *Wiring a Continent* (1947), Western Union's services proved of much use to the economy. "The businessman, the banker, the broker, and the capitalist were enabled to operate upon a constantly broadening basis," Thompson commented, "as it became feasible to reach out over hundreds or even thousands of miles and obtain intelligence within a matter of minutes. The increased scope of the operations which the telegraph made possible was a significant factor in the development of big business and the rise of finance capitalism." The appearance of the telephone later in the century further increased the ease of communications, but the telegraph was the truly revolutionary invention. The great advances that came with the introduction of the speed of electronic communications through the medium of the telegraph opened new worlds to the potential empire builder.

The improvements in transportation and communication permitted the creation of the first mass marketers in the closing decades of the nineteenth century. These included the large department stores in major cities, the great mail-order houses such as Montgomery Ward, Sears, and the Larkin Company, as well as the first chain stores. The development of mass retailing represented a major step toward a more homogeneous nation, which further hastened the decline of the older society. (We will consider the cultural impact of mass marketing in the next chapter.) By and large, the mass marketers sold goods from the older sectors of the economy, industries in which some of the distribution could be handled more effectively by the mass marketing specialists rather than by the traditional web of wholesalers and retailers.

The third and final precondition for the spread of big business outside the realm of transportation and communications was the appearance of an array of technological advances in manufacturing technology. As JoAnne Yates wrote in *Control through Communication* (1989), "the spread of the telegraph and of railroads . . . encouraged firms to serve larger, regional and national markets, while improvements in manufacturing technology created potential economies of scale." Many of those improvements came in the generation of new products or new processes for making old ones. In industry after industry in the closing decades of the nineteenth century, technological improvements made it possible to lower the costs of production dramatically. Larger plants employing mass-production technologies could for the first time turn out quality goods in such volumes that businesses then turned to building complex managerial systems to plan and coordinate their production and distribution. Advances in the techniques for making iron and steel and other metals, for example, and for shaping and working them, made available powerful new machines that increased output. In an interrelated set of industries, as David A. Hounshell showed in *From the American System to Mass Production, 1800–1932* (1984), highly specialized machines for manufacture, finishing, and assembly brought vastly increased productivity. At the same time, as Alfred Chandler emphasized in *The Visible Hand* (1977), some manufacturers utilized increased amounts of heat (primarily from coal) in their production processes. In other sectors new energy sources such as petroleum and electricity fueled new industries. Advances in refining and distilling techniques called forth astonishing improvements in output and soon led to the establishment of the best known of the early mass producers, Standard Oil. As the numbers of factories increased, so did the problems in managing them. Soon a whole generation of engineers turned their energies to the task of better organizing factory production, a development known initially as *systematic management* and later as *scientific management*. "As the new mass production industries became capital-intensive and management-intensive," wrote Alfred Chandler, "the resulting increase in fixed costs and the desire to keep their machinery or workers and managerial staff fully employed created pressures on the owners and managers." Soon they were led along the first of the major paths to big business in manufacturing.

Vertical Growth

In the years before the beginning of the great merger movement in 1895, big business arrived in the nation's manufacturing sector in two broadly defined ways. One was growth of a single firm via vertical integration, wherein the owners of a business would perceive a large potential market and find that to reach that market effectively, they had to engage in new functions. That is, the business could not simply produce goods but had to do other things as well, such as move into the marketing of the goods. A big business usually engaged in a number of different activities, such as purchasing or growing its raw materials, fabricating those materials into goods, transporting its own products, wholesaling them, or even taking care of retailing them to consumers. A firm that did a number of different things was said to be vertically integrated because it handled the necessary activities on various rungs of the ladder reaching from raw materials all the way up to final consumers. If a company started out just as a producer of goods and then moved into marketing, it was said to have integrated *forward,* that is, closer to the final rung. And if it moved into owning its raw material sources, it had integrated *backward,* that is, further away from the functions at the top of the ladder. Some firms grew to be big businesses by expanding vertically (usually into marketing) and achieving such success that they became large and powerful corporations. We will refer to this pattern of becoming or creating a big business as *vertical growth.*

The other general method by which big businesses arose was *horizontal growth.* In that case, a number of producers who all did the same thing would join to form a combination of their interests. That kind of firm had formed horizontally rather than vertically, because it was an amalgamation of firms that all engaged only in production or transportation or marketing; the newly born combination was usually not engaged in the full range of activities on the vertical rungs of the ladder. Instead it arose through a combination of similar businesses, all sharing the same rung on the industry ladder. When people spoke of "the trusts" around the turn of the century, they usually were thinking of the companies that began by this method of horizontal growth. We will examine horizontal growth in more detail later.

Although the terms help one conceptualize the changes, this general division of the rise of big business through vertical and horizontal growth oversimplifies matters. Numerous large enterprises of the period grew through a combination of the two methods, and one could cite exceptions to the overall descriptions of either growth process. Nevertheless, the general interpretation of the two paths to bigness, vertical and horizontal, explains much about the rise of big business. Alfred D. Chandler's pathbreak-ing article in the *Business History Review* (Spring 1959), "The Beginnings of 'Big Business' in American Industry," was the first study to emphasize the vertical route to large-scale organization. Previous historians had concentrated on the horizontal combinations, but the usefulness of Chandler's more inclusive framework has been widely accepted.

The big businesses that arose primarily through vertical growth were a mixed lot, more difficult to analyze than the horizontal combinations. Perhaps the most effective way to explain the process of vertical expansion is to say that these businesses usually began as producers and, in the course of increasing the scale of their operations, found shortcomings in the existing mechanisms by which they obtained raw materials or sold finished goods. Those shortcomings led them to integrate backward or forward into functions they had not performed initially. And in the process of meeting a new demand more efficiently through integration, some businesses managed to evolve into very large firms. These companies usually grew without significant mergers, at least for some years, expanding to greater size primarily on the basis of vertical growth. Their success often led others to follow their lead, and it was important to be an early competitor if not the real innovator who assembled resources in a new way. The successful innovations of one company often drew imitators, and such industries usually came to be dominated by several large firms. That kind of industry, characterized by a relatively few large companies, is called an *oligopoly*. Many of the nation's industries in the center economy were oligopolies by the early twentieth century, and such concentrations of production among a relatively small number of firms in one industry comprised companies built by horizontal as well as by vertical growth.

Manufacturers who pioneered in the building of large, vertically integrated companies had usually encountered problems either in marketing their goods or in acquiring their supplies. Marketing was the more important of the two problems, at least in terms of generating massive corporations. The older merchandising system was one in which almost all manufactured goods except those sold to local customers were marketed through independent wholesale merchants. This same web of commercial agents tied the economy together, gathering goods from a number of producers and distributing them to a diffuse market of relatively small and scattered buyers. The independent merchants also extended credit to manufacturers, arranged for the transportation of goods, and performed other services, all of which made them the wealthiest and most powerful group of business figures in the country. They played vital roles in encouraging manufactures and in backing internal improvements in transportation and communications. The merchants' control over marketing rested on the nature of products and of markets, as well as on an intimate knowledge of their suppliers and customers. Independent wholesalers met the needs of manufacturers very well as long as the products in which they dealt required only storage and shipping, without special complications in transport or handling.

Once products appeared that called for special handling or particular marketing expertise, however, the merchants proved less useful. Both perishable and technologically complex goods presented real difficulties for a marketing network geared to items that stored fairly well for long periods and that necessitated no expertise or demonstrations. Goods that called for new marketing techniques appeared in a number of industries in the last half of the nineteenth century and the early years of the twentieth. The changes in the nature of products sometimes led innovative producers to integrate forward because they could handle their own merchandising better than could the old mercantile system. Producers also found direct contacts with customers useful for acquiring better information on how to improve products and services.

Similarly, alterations in manufacturers' needs for raw materials or semifinished products encouraged some firms to integrate backward toward those sources. In the antebellum economy, manufacturers had learned to live with the difficulties of procuring supplies through independent merchants. Once businesses began to produce on a larger scale, with a range of interdependent activities, they felt vulnerable because they had so little control over their supply sources. Mass production called for a steady stream of large quantities of raw materials at relatively predictable and acceptable prices. The old fluctuations in supply (and consequently in cost) became less tolerable. In order to assure themselves of adequate supplies of raw materials at reasonably stable prices, thereby smoothing the flow of materials through the production and distribution process, some manufacturers integrated backward. Makers of iron and steel, for example, bought lands with metal deposits or coal to guard against the ups and downs of the open market in iron ore or fuels. Another reason for backward integration was to achieve a more-uniform quality of raw materials. The latter case was most frequent in industries that relied on technologically complex or science-based production, such as the refining of petroleum and the manufacturing of iron and steel. Backward integration, then, was seen both as a means of gaining more control over erratic markets and as a way to improve quality control. It also was an important means of preventing the entry of competitors, who often had to seek new sources of supply to compete effectively with established firms.

Integration became a key element in the growing effort to substitute what Alfred Chandler called the visible hand of management for the erratic, uncontrolled, invisible hand of the market. By integrating their operations, firms could not only enjoy efficient operation (*economies of scale*) with large, productive facilities, but improvements through the integration of other functions as well, sometimes known as *economies of scope.* They also increased their market power in the process, sometimes reaping excessive profits in the short run. By examining in a bit more detail the experience of several giant businesses that appeared through vertical growth, we will be able to understand this route to bigness better.

One of the most striking illustrations of the coming of big business via vertical growth is the history of the meatpacking industry. In the decades before the 1870s, beef was produced and consumed largely on a local basis. Thus the meatpacking business initially consisted of numerous relatively small companies that slaughtered and packed pork in the great midwestern centers of the industry, especially Cincinnati and Chicago. Packers would cure the pork or ship it in brine over considerable distances. When the long-distance trade in beef began, however, it was handled differently. Beef was not cured or pickled, and the meat did not stay fresh for very long after slaughtering, so cattle were shipped on the hoof by rail from the midwestern stockyard centers such as Omaha, Kansas City, and Chicago.

The railroads built vast, widespread facilities to handle the movement of cattle from the West to the urban centers in the East. Once the animals reached their destination, local butchers slaughtered and sold them. A great opportunity awaited the entrepreneur who could devise and implement a more efficient way to handle this trade.

That person turned out to be Gustavus Swift. Swift perceived (as did a few others) that considerable savings could be achieved if the cattle could be slaughtered and prepared in the midwestern stockyard areas and then shipped to distant markets. At the western end, large numbers of animals could be systematically and efficiently butchered in large-scale slaughterhouses, which would reduce the costs of preparing the beef for market. More savings would result when the product was shipped because only ready-to-market meat (called dressed beef) would be transported, not the entire animal with its inedible parts as well as the meat. The success of any such plan depended first on improvements in the technology of refrigeration, and Swift watched with interest the early experimental shipments of dressed beef in the 1870s. The imperfect refrigerated rail cars of those years, as shown in Oscar E. Anderson's *Refrigeration in America* (1953), quickly gave way to much better, more reliable ones.

Swift, who had come to Chicago in 1875 as a buyer for a Boston meat concern, soon became convinced that with improved refrigeration he could successfully market dressed beef. In 1878 he formed a new business, attempting to implement his ideas. The concern faced numerous problems in displacing the old set of arrangements among shippers, eastern butchers, and the railroads, which had substantial investments in facilities to handle the movement of live cattle. Indeed, the railroads sought to block Swift's new business because it represented a fundamentally different way of operating the beef business and thus threatened their investment in the old technology of distributing beef. By exploiting the competition between the railroads, as Mary Yeager's *Competition and Regulation: The Development of Oligopoly in the Meat Packing Industry* (1981) demonstrated, Swift was able to get his products shipped by rail to eastern cit-

ies in his own refrigerated cars. The real problem, though, lay
with the distribution network.

In order to make his plans work, Swift needed not only
shipping facilities but refrigerated warehouses to store the beef
once it arrived. Again, the old order of the railroads and the local butchers had no incentive to create such facilities. Swift
could not simply have the beef unloaded on the streets of New
York on a summer's day and then wait for buyers. The existing
wholesale marketing arrangements for fresh meat were of no
use to him, because they did not include the refrigerated facilities he required. He was thus forced to build a network of
branch houses to store and sell chilled beef. During the 1880s,
Swift & Company created a nationwide web of the necessary
facilities, often forming partnerships with local jobbers willing
to join the new venture. Once Swift overcame initial consumer
resistance to meat slaughtered days before in distant places, his
products found a booming market because they proved to be
just as good as freshly butchered meats and were substantially
cheaper.

After Swift's integration into marketing, the company quickly
became a complex big business. The firm's purchases of live animals, the activities of its large slaughtering and butchering
plants in the Midwest, and the transport of its dressed beef all
had to be coordinated very carefully to match the fluctuating
demand in the cities where the meat was consumed. Swift &
Company was an early user of telegraph services to allow rapid
communication between its far-flung operations. Before the
merger wave of the 1890s, the firm had created a vertically integrated big business as a result of the expansion into marketing
made necessary by the shortcomings of the existing distribution
network, exposed by the introduction of a new and better idea.

Swift's success quickly attracted imitators anxious to cash
in on the new trade. By the 1890s, competitors like Philip
Armour had followed on Swift's heels and carved out a share of
the market by building similar, integrated businesses. It was not,
however, a game that very many could play successfully. The
size of the market was large but not infinite, and there was a

premium on getting in early. This meant that the industry would likely be dominated by a few large firms rather than by many small enterprises as in the older order. It was to become a common pattern in many industries.

Critics soon began including the "Beef Trust" on their list of concentrated industries. The giant meatpackers became the target of one of the era's earliest "muckrakers," Upton Sinclair. In his novel *The Jungle* (1906), Sinclair portrayed the drudgery and hopelessness of the slaughterhouse workers and sounded a plea for socialism, dedicating his book to the workers of America. Most public criticism focused not on working conditions in the industry, but on health issues and on the collusion of big packers. The results of a federal investigation published in 1905 (the *Report of the Commissioner of Corporations on the Beef Industry*), though, indicated relatively little evidence of illegal activity by Swift and other meatpackers. Although the packers remained targets of regulators thereafter, it seems clear that they had not achieved their initial success and evolved into giant enterprises principally by absorbing or colluding with other meatpackers—instead, they had grown through internal expansion begun by integration into marketing.

Another firm that rose to national significance after integrating forward to market a perishable item was the United Fruit Company. That firm experienced its growth during the height of the merger movement at the turn of the century, but it was not created by horizontal merger. Its history closely parallels that of Swift & Company and is a good illustration of vertical growth. United Fruit grew into a major business by making a new "product"—the banana—available to consumers in the United States. Before the Civil War, bananas were not sold in American markets, but by the end of the 1860s some shipments had begun to arrive in port cities. Because of its highly perishable nature, it could not be sold in interior regions. Even after steamships were introduced in the 1870s and 1880s to speed the hauling of fruit from the Caribbean, the poor marketing facilities inland largely restricted consumption of bananas to the coastal cities. The commercial produce network in the nation's interior lacked adequate warehouses refrigerated (for summers) and heated (for winters). The innovator who followed Swift's pattern to create a national market was a Bostonian named Andrew W. Preston.

Preston helped create the United Fruit Company in 1899, and as its first president he worked to build an integrated business that could overcome the shortcomings of the existing marketing system. The firm created a nationwide network of wholesale houses equipped with the necessary cooling and heating apparatus to allow sales in many areas. Within two years, distributing outlets were opened in twenty-one major cities, and business was booming. Within ten years of its creation, United Fruit had become one of the country's major corporations and boasted more than $40 million in assets. Although no Upton Sinclair appeared to write a novel depicting the less admirable aspects of its operations, United Fruit later became a symbol of United States economic imperialism, exercising great political and economic influence in what Americans sometimes condescendingly referred to as the banana republics of Latin America.

Marketing and coordination problems led others besides the purveyors of perishable goods into vertical integration. Early firms in the electrical industry, for example, created major businesses primarily through internal expansion and vertical integration. An intelligent strategy of integration was only one of the factors that explained the success of the industry's two giants, General Electric and Westinghouse. As Harold C. Passer's *The Electrical Manufacturers, 1875–1900* (1953) argued, both mergers and the advantages of monopoly control of production resulting from the patent laws played important parts. However, the two firms that dominated the industry by the early twentieth century could never have grown large if they had not taken the initiative in marketing to overcome the inadequacy of the existing system.

Though its origins lay in the preceding decade, the electrical industry emerged as a significant business in the 1880s. Thomas Edison's enterprises began in 1879 and expanded in subsequent years, producing both heavy industrial machinery to generate and transmit electrical energy and lamps to convert the new energy source into light. The several Edison businesses were combined in 1889 to form the Edison General Electric Company, which in turn became one of the two firms that joined to spawn the General Electric Company in 1892. The other firm was the Thomson-Houston Electric Company, begun in 1882. General Electric's great American rival, Westinghouse, was founded in 1884 by George Westinghouse. All these early electrical manufacturers encountered very difficult problems in introducing a new product so technologically complex that the existing marketing system of independent wholesalers could not handle it well. The new industry found two major kinds of markets for its products. One was the growing number of central stations that generated and transmitted electricity to a group of local customers. This first market was the early form of what would later grow into the vast economic, technical, and social systems represented by giant electric utility complexes throughout the Western world, as analyzed in Thomas P. Hughes's *Networks of Power* (1983). The other early market was the "isolated system," in which a factory, store, or home had its own generator and internal lighting or electrically driven machinery, rather than drawing power from a central station. In either case the traditional merchandising channels simply did not work well in meeting the particular needs of the equipment manufacturers.

The merchandising difficulties sprang fundamentally from the new technological challenges associated with the product. First, the products were quite costly and highly dangerous in the hands of people who did not understand their use and maintenance. A number of disastrous fires, injuries, and deaths marred the early years of the industry because of the considerable destructive potential of electrical energy. It would not do simply to ship equipment to a customer and hope for the best, because any resulting tragedy would constitute what the president of Thomson-Houston called in 1887 "a serious drawback" to the wider introduction of electricity. The only satisfactory solution was to integrate forward into marketing by creating special departments to handle the installation of the goods, instruct the customers thoroughly in the proper operation of the apparatus, and take care of repairing the systems when necessary. Because the industry was so new, the manufacturers themselves had to take the initiative and supply a body of trained personnel to provide the necessary expertise and service.

The other technological difficulty lay in the particular needs of individual customers. Because the requirements of buyers were often unique or highly specialized (especially in cases where the electrical machinery was to be used to supply power for manufacturing), it was essential to have a well-trained force of company engineers to consult closely with potential customers. Westinghouse met this requirement by establishing, in the company's earliest days, a subsidiary engineering firm to market its products. Thomson-Houston (before it became part of GE) and Edison General Electric found it essential to supply similar services in the 1880s. By the end of that decade, the three major electrical companies had all established national marketing systems with sales offices and trained personnel who had the vital expertise to secure orders, install and operate equipment safely, and follow up with repair services and assistance. The same pattern would be followed in the twentieth century by other high-technology enterprises such as IBM.

As the history of the early electrical manufacturers showed, in new industries with extraordinary marketing needs it was often likely that producers would find themselves creating large, complex, vertically integrated enterprises. Even when the goods did fit reasonably comfortably into existing channels, producers often created their own distribution networks because this improved their communication with their customers and thus could lead to better service and new products. Expansion and the assumption of additional economic functions as a result of similar shortcomings in the old distribution network characterized firms in a number of other industries in the last half of the nineteenth century and the early years of the twentieth. Pioneering makers of such goods as harvesters, sewing machines, heavy industrial machinery of various kinds, and new office machines such as adding machines, typewriters, and cash registers often found it necessary to supply such services as demonstrations, consumer credit, and repairs. In many cases the manufacturers found the existing marketing network too passive a means of pushing new goods into the marketplace; independent merchants were not accustomed to providing aggressive sales techniques and service on behalf of their many suppliers. In order to exert more control over the introduction of their new and complex goods in an often indifferent marketplace, producers found it desirable to integrate forward and assume a more active and multifaceted role in distribution. When, for example, the automobile industry appeared after 1900, producers found that similar problems forced them to assert some control over dealers to assure the proper introduction, aggressive sales strategies, credit arrangements, and repair facilities in order to market what was then a completely new, costly, and technologically complex product.

The explosive growth of these innovative and expansive companies, such as the Singer sewing machine firm, also helped pave the way for big business by removing some potential legal barriers at the state level. As legal historian Charles W. McCurdy established, it had long been possible for states to discourage competition from out-of-state firms by creating costly regulations or taxing their operations. As the new firms such as Singer and Swift fought such obstacles, they eventually persuaded the courts that those efforts amounted to a form of internal tariffs and were thus illegal, since the commerce clause of the Constitution said that only the federal government could regulate commerce. By about 1890, the courtroom successes of vertically integrated giants such as Singer had extended the commerce clause to create a national market in legal terms. As McCurdy put it, to support American economic progress, the United States Supreme Court assumed the role of "umpire of the nation's free-trade network."

Some big businesses grew partly in response to shortcomings in the system for supplying raw materials. Considerable vertical integration existed, for example, in the steel industry by the early 1890s. Andrew Carnegie's steel enterprises led the way toward integration during the 1870s and 1880s, as Joseph Frazier Wall's *Andrew Carnegie* (1970) demonstrated. Carnegie marshaled capital and invested it in the latest, most technologically advanced production facilities. The dominance of his company rested on its ability to produce at lower costs than his competitors. To achieve that position, Carnegie's enterprises operated on a huge scale and engaged in considerable backward integration. Steel was made from pig iron, and Carnegie resolved by the 1870s to control much of his own supply of that raw material. Fluctuations in the quantity, price, and quality of pig iron bought on the open market led the Carnegie businesses to produce their own supplies to feed their Bessemer converters, which in turn fed their rolling mills. Through the efforts of Carnegie's partner, Henry Clay Frick, they soon moved even further backward, acquiring their own sources of iron ore, coal, and coke for fuel. Carnegie Steel even had its own fleet of steamships and a company railroad to transport its materials. James H. Bridge marveled in his *Inside History of the Carnegie Steel Company* (1903) that "from the moment these crude stuffs were dug out of the earth until they flowed in a stream of liquid steel in the ladles, there was never a price, profit, or royalty paid to an outsider." Because they found that they could assure themselves of a steady, reliable flow of raw materials and semifinished goods at low prices by integrating backward, producers like Carnegie sometimes expanded into new functions in order to make themselves, as Carnegie himself put it, more nearly "independent of the general market." In handling the enormously complicated tasks of coordinating, overseeing, and evaluating the activities of his many interrelated enterprises, Carnegie made good use of his knowledge of management and accounting practices first worked out on the railroads, as Harold C. Livesay argued in *Andrew Carnegie and the Rise of Big Business* (1975). Other steelmakers soon followed Carnegie's lead into integration and the adoption of the modern managerial and accounting practices necessary to keep track of such varied and large-scale undertakings as a steel-manufacturing enterprise.

As large, vertically integrated businesses developed in the American economy, they assumed a wide range of new functions and at the same time aroused fear and bitter complaints about their size and power. Nonetheless, collusion and conspiracy—though often sought but only occasionally sustained—do not seem to explain much of the success these giant companies enjoyed. Most of these early vertically built enterprises grew big without significant benefit of mergers or long-term, effective collusive behavior. In many instances, such as the cases of Swift and the electrical manufacturers, they supplied new and better products to a nation that embraced them as further evidence that theirs was an age of great progress. In a number of other instances, products such as those of the steel industry were not only better than the ones they replaced, but they were offered at steadily lower prices, thereby benefiting consumers. One might condemn, as many did, the fact that workers did not share more of the resulting profits. One might note that competition often unfolded on less than an even playing field. One might also argue that the entrepreneurs received more than a satisfactory reward, as they reaped wealth on a scale not seen previously by private citizens. Nevertheless, the pioneering big businesses that arose through vertical growth appeared to owe their success primarily to just the sort of creativity, drive, and cost-consciousness that Americans professed to admire and always had tended to reward in their economic system. That is, however, considerably less true of many of the big businesses created through horizontal growth.

Horizontal Growth

The successful businesses that had their origins in horizontal mergers before 1895 went through a roughly common set of experiences. First, a number of manufacturers would enter an industry (often a new industry), producing goods in volume in factories that sometimes required quite substantial capital investment. For a time, all would be well. Profits would be good, and the businesses would expand, often leading others to enter the industry to share in the promise of prosperity. As the market began to fill up, however, producers found that they had to compete vigorously in order to keep or enlarge their share of the market. Most manufacturers tried to do so by cutting the prices on their goods. After a period of sharp price competition (usually described as "ruinous" or at least "destructive" by the business leaders), they would find that profits and prices were not meeting their expectations and begin to search for a solution to this problem.

Since most of those in the business world, like human beings in general, are prone to look for solutions that require the least possible change from their previous situations, they first looked for a way out that would allow them to remain separate, independent businesses. The basic problem they were trying to overcome was the difficulty of regulating production levels and prices in order to assure steady profits, as noted by many studies then and later, such as the essays in William Z. Ripley, ed., *Trusts, Pools and Corporations* (1905). If everyone would just behave properly, restricting output and maintaining prices, the days of comfortable profits might be restored. So, like the railroads before them, manufacturers turned to American versions of the cartel, a loose form of organizational control that seemed to hold out the promise of halting the overproduction and falling prices while at the same time allowing each producer to remain independent. Cartel behavior took many shapes, including so-called "gentlemen's agreements," pools, and the most common form, the trade association. Producers of, for example, steel rails could join together to form a Steel Rail Association to provide a convenient format in which they might agree to fix prices, set output quotas, or divide the market in some manner, such as by apportioning geographic territories among the members of the association.

From the point of view of the manufacturers involved, there were at least two things wrong with the association solution. One was that such arrangements were political lightning rods. After the Sherman Act became law in 1890 in response to that political reaction, such cartel-like behavior was of highly questionable legality. Perhaps a more important shortcoming was that the associations did not work very well. Although they tried various ways to enforce the decisions of the group, most producers ultimately found that there was no consistently effective way to do so. A few producers usually stayed out of the association, thereby undermining the efforts of those member firms. Furthermore, the agreements were strictly voluntary, not legally binding contracts. Under the common-law tradition it was not illegal to make such agreements, but they were deemed hostile enough to the public interest that they were denied the protection afforded by the law to contracts. They could have worked only if the participants had strictly and voluntarily lived up to the terms set by the associations. But the temptation to cut prices and to try to conceal that fact by paying secret rebates to wholesalers or to other customers was eventually too strong for many allied producers. Downward fluctuations in business conditions often flushed out at least one greedy or weak manufacturer who wanted more than had been allotted to it in the pool. Another problem was that initially successful associations sometimes lured new producers, eager to join in the good times, into the industry. Their productive capacity could prove the last straw, bringing prices and profits down again. In this light the associations were, in the terse and contemptuous judgment of John D. Rockefeller, "ropes of sand."

Margaret Levenstein's work on closely related elements of the early chemical industry (in the *Journal of Economic History,* 1995), illustrated the difficulties that caused most of the collusive efforts such as pools to fail. The producers of salt, for instance, experienced problems common to many industries over the course of the nineteenth century. Initially these manufacturers were "balkanized by high transportation costs" and therefore more or less insulated from competition. But as the century progressed, "transport costs fell and markets expanded geographically," and the competition became fierce. Because there were no great technological improvements in production, and because raw material sources were plentiful, barriers to entry into the industry were low. Under such conditions, output rose and prices fell. This led manufacturers to try pools, in which they sought to fix prices and limit output, often using "creative and persistent" arrangements. But because there were no effective barriers to entry either in production or distribution—salt was a generic product, making it difficult to establish brands or higher-quality versions of the goods—these pools "remained largely unsuccessful." Whenever pools in a particular industry did succeed in the short run, higher prices quickly led new competitors to enter, and the pools "always broke down within a year or two." Remarkably, "although total output" in the salt industry "quadrupled between 1880 and 1896, the real value of total output stayed almost the same," as manufacturers ran ever harder to stay in the same place.

But pools were not always failures. In the fine-chemical manufacturing industry (which processed and marketed pharmaceuticals and similar goods), pools sometimes remained successful for longer periods of time, as Levenstein's analysis of the small chemical bromine industry showed. There, pools could erect effective barriers at the distribution and marketing end of the business.

In a relatively small number of industries before 1895, some firms took the next step after the failure of pools and associations: an attempt at horizontal combination. Here, all or many of the major producers in an industry would form a single firm, at least in the legal sense. The first form in which this occurred was the trust, pioneered in 1882 by Rockefeller's Standard Oil. In that form of organization, a group of trustees (leading producers in the industry) received and held the common stock of different corporations in exchange for trust certificates, thereby effecting legal control by the trust over the properties of the participating firms. This legal device attempted to bypass the common-law prohibition against one corporation holding stock in another without explicit statutory authority from a state legislature.

After 1889 it became easier to form a horizontal combination by incorporating in New Jersey, which enacted a general incorporation law permitting corporations chartered there to own stock in other such businesses without any need for special legislative action. It was theoretically possible for other states to block these combinations by preventing businesses chartered in their states from selling out to or cooperating with the combine, as legal historian Charles W. McCurdy pointed out. But as a practical matter the states were reluctant to do so, as this would have required them to give up some benefits of the large corporations and would in effect have led the states into economic planning. They could in theory forbid local businesses to sell out to New Jersey–chartered corporations, but they could hardly then compel them to stay in business, or tell them how to operate their businesses thereafter. For the states to act so aggressively, even against hated out-of-state combinations, was unlikely. That would have been seen as an unacceptable interference with private property rights.

With the removal of many potential legal barriers, an increasing number of industries put combinations together as holding companies rather than as trusts—a legal distinction all but ignored by the public at the time as well as by many historians later. The popularity of the word *trust* resulted in its being used to denote holding companies as well as much looser business alliances such as pools and associations. By achieving the legal status of trusts or holding companies, the new horizontal combinations found themselves in a much stronger position to control the pricing and output decisions of their constituent parts, and to begin to build new administrative networks to manage the giant enterprises.

Once the leading producers had formed a combine, however, the new corporation often functioned for a time as a loose amalgam of divisions, each of which retained much of its former autonomy. This situation in fact amounted to a continuation of the pattern of cartel-like behavior, because the firm's new central office often exercised little effective control and direction other than acting as a general forum in which to decide prices, output, and how to apportion the market. If all went well for the combination, and the profits turned out as hoped, this loose kind of corporation might continue for a time. If, however, trouble appeared in the form of competition from old "outside" producers who had refused to give up their independence by joining the combination, or from new competitors (sometimes foreign concerns), the combination was usually forced to take away the autonomy of its subdivisions and exercise more unified control from the central office. Often the most effective way to maintain market position and profits was to become more competitive by ordering the closing of the less-efficient plants, or by integrating forward or backward to perform marketing functions better or obtain raw materials more reliably or more cheaply. In this way, many of the firms that started as loose, horizontal combinations evolved into vertically integrated, centrally administered businesses. Some remained loose combinations for a few years, and others collapsed and disappeared from the roll of American corporations. Most of the successful combinations, however, did become vertically integrated big businesses. If they could not do so, as in the case of the Whiskey Trust, for example, they usually failed outright or lost market share to new competitors. The general horizontal growth pattern just described was the road taken by a number of large-scale enterprises created before 1895 and by the great majority of the giant corporations built in the years after 1895—in the most explosive phase of the merger movement.

The decline of prices was extremely important in the process outlined above, and one should bear in mind the general movement in price levels in the long stretch from the end of the Civil War to around 1895. An important study of prices was done by G. F. Warren and F. A. Pearson, appearing in their short monograph *Wholesale Prices for 213 Years: 1720–1932* and in their book called *Prices* (1933), both based largely on data for New York City. Those studies and others demonstrated a broad, fairly steady decline in prices from the end of the Civil War to the mid-1890s. The wholesale price index for all commodities in 1866 (according to the Warren and Pearson studies) stood at 174; by 1870 it was down to 135, by 1880 to 100, and by 1890 to 82, or less than half of what it was at the close of the Civil War. Of course the pattern of declining prices was not continuous; in some years prices did increase. But as difficult as it may be for us to imagine today, the overall pattern for thirty years was definitely one of falling prices. The wholesale costs of every major category of goods—farm products, food, leather, textiles, fuels, metals, building materials, drugs and chemicals, household goods, and distilled spirits—fell considerably during the years that brought the beginnings of big business. The experience of the salt industry, mentioned above, was typical. When manufacturers complained bitterly about plummeting prices and declining profits, it is clear that they were at least correct about prices.

Those falling prices were largely a reflection of improvements in transportation and declining costs of production brought on by the spread of mass-production techniques. Before about 1870, as Lance E. Davis and Douglass C. North pointed out in their *Institutional Change and American Economic Growth* (1971), most industries were subject to what economists call "constant returns to scale," which simply means that while a bigger factory would allow the production of more goods, the costs per unit of output were about the same for large as for small producers. In many important industries after the Civil War, however, technological changes brought "economies of scale." This meant that a large, expensive plant could produce more cheaply on a per-unit basis than could a smaller one, as long as the large plant operated at high levels of output. The Bessemer process of steelmaking, for example, brought economies of scale to big producers in that industry. Other examples included petroleum refining and flour milling. Since such industries almost always saw the growth of highly capital-intensive production, the firms involved experienced high fixed costs somewhat similar to those encountered earlier on the railroads. Economies of scale, coupled with improved management techniques and the existence of highly competitive conditions in many industries, pushed prices down.

It is not difficult to imagine the cumulative psychological effect of this long price decline on producers. During the six decades before the Civil War, prices had not behaved in such a manner. Falling prices and periodic panics had occurred, of course, but never so relentlessly for such a long time. This steady downward trend in prices received for manufactured goods disturbed and unnerved many in the business world. It was doubtless an element in encouraging them to turn increasingly toward cooperation rather than competition, and it helps explain the widespread tendency in so many branches of manufacturing to search for ways of controlling output and prices.

In many industries, especially new ones or ones that enjoyed some kind of significant improvements in the technology of production, manufacturers initially found themselves in an enviable position. Growth was rapid and profits were good as the producers expanded to meet the demands for their product. Eventually, however, demand leveled off as the manufacturers grew to the point where they turned out as much as (and often more than) the market wanted. Then problems set in as firms struggled for a larger share of what had suddenly become an increasingly stable or much more slowly growing market. At this point, profits might actually decline or disappear, and manufacturers were likely to believe themselves in trouble and start searching for a solution.

A brief look at one minor industry, the manufacture of wire nails, will help to illustrate the above pattern. Until the 1880s, almost all nails used in the United States were flat nails cut from metal plates. By that decade, however, a number of new competitors making round nails out of wire had appeared and gained ground rapidly, with production levels rising steeply. By the middle of the 1890s, the lower-cost wire nails had almost replaced cut nails in that market. Nonetheless, the early growth and profits in wire nails began to level off, and producers suddenly found their situation less satisfactory. Recalling the years prior to 1895, one analyst of the nail industry wrote in 1897 that the "manufacturers had been fairly contented, making the comfortable profits of a new and rapidly growing business." When the pace of profit growth declined, however, the producers "cried out with one voice that they were ruined by competition." The first result of manufacturers' subsequent initiatives was not a genuine trust or combination, but an association of independent wire nail makers seeking to set pooling arrangements to fix prices and output. For a short time after the arrangement began, prices did rise. But soon thereafter prices declined again, and the pool collapsed. The experience of makers of wire nails was typical of many other new industries after the Civil War.

To some extent it may be argued that almost all industries that relied on factory or mass production went through something like the above pattern. In the textile industry, the nation's first factory-dominated branch of manufacturing, Louis Galambos's *Competition and Cooperation* (1966) showed that the earliest attempts at forming trade associations came in the 1850s, a time of declining profits. Because the factory or mass-production techniques did not come to many other industries until after the mid 1840s or 1850s, one might anticipate that the period of good, growing profits in those industries would have lasted until about the 1860s. The depression of the 1870s, coupled with the onset of falling prices after the Civil War, put strong pressure on manufacturers and probably accounted for the fact that the first widespread attempts by manufacturers to form pools and associations came in that decade. The search for reliable methods of controlling prices and output and therefore profits continued into the early years of the twentieth century, and it was especially common in new industries and in those that underwent significant technological changes and rapid growth.

It was just such industries, as Naomi R. Lamoreaux argued in *The Great Merger Movement in American Business, 1895–1904* (1985), that were the likeliest ones to form horizontal combinations under the stress of the depression of the 1890s. Lamoreaux emphasized that those industries were generally not characterized by *robber barons* or by highly creative entrepreneurs. Unlike many earlier manufacturers, they were committed primarily to "running full and steady," and there were generally fewer and larger competing firms in these industries than in many of the older ones. These mass production–oriented businesses constituted what Lamoreaux called a "new industrial structure," one particularly sensitive to the pressure of falling prices. Though not dominated by such compelling figures as the industrial giants that the public damned as robber barons, these lesser peers would follow a number of the organizational paths blazed by the pioneers.

During the three decades after 1865, then, manufacturers in industry after industry found their profits or growth rates unsatisfactory and turned to various forms of cartel-like behavior for an answer. Sometimes that behavior took the form of an informal pool for higher prices, lower production levels, or apportioned markets. Sometimes it manifested itself in a trade association, a somewhat more formal means of cooperation, yet one that still left each firm an independent entity, free in the end to pursue its own course if it chose to do so. Sometimes (after the formation of Standard Oil in 1882), it went so far as to result in a true, legally unified trust or holding company that saw the surrender of autonomy by previously independent businesses. In contemporary public thought, all such attempts at cooperation were simply the *trusts*, the catchall term for any apparent concentration of economic power. Organizational changes involving the surrender of legal autonomy were generally the ones that led to the kinds of firms that defined big business in the early years of the twentieth century.

Among the industries that between 1865 and 1895 definitely engaged in some form of cartel-like behavior were the following: textiles, iron and steel, nonferrous metals, hardware, petroleum, sugar refineries, tobacco manufacturers, lumber, anthracite coal, salt, leather products, cottonseed oil, liquor, glass, paper, and gunpowder. The attempts at cooperation often began on a state or regional level and then expanded to a national scale. Once businesses in a number of industries began to experiment with cartel behavior, others began to try it as a means of improving their economic position. In the 1880s and early 1890s, however, relatively few industries produced real trusts or holding companies that proved to be lasting, successful firms that became vertically integrated, complex big businesses. We will briefly examine three of the industries in which cartel-like behavior did result in a trust or a holding company before 1895 to see in more detail how the process worked. The three combinations we will look at—in oil, sugar, and tobacco—played important roles in creating and publicizing the immensely profitable road manufacturers might travel if they could form a genuinely unified, legally binding "trust." The success of these companies (and a few others) helped to pave the way for the flood of mergers after that date by fostering a widespread thirst to build combinations, a thirst satisfied in the turn-of-the-century merger movement.

The pioneer enterprise in the story of industrial combinations was Standard Oil. Ida Tarbell, in her *History of the Standard Oil Company* (1904), succinctly summarized the importance of the rise of that firm: "It was the first in the field, and it has furnished the methods, the charter, and the traditions of its followers." Standard was the first great horizontal combination in manufacturing, and no other company has been the subject of so many historical inquiries for so many decades. Henry Demarest Lloyd's passionate *Wealth Against Commonwealth* (1894) set the tone for most of the subsequent highly critical interpretations. Of the later studies, the two most thoroughly researched (and more sympathetic) works were Ralph and Muriel Hidy, *Pioneering in Big Business, 1882–1911* (1955) and Harold F. Williamson, Arnold R. Daum, and others, *The American Petroleum Industry: The Age of Illumination, 1859–1899* (1959). The evolution of Standard Oil, as all historians who have studied it have demonstrated, was a protracted struggle by John D. Rockefeller and his associates to bring order and stability to an unruly industry by imposing centralized control, discouraging competition, whereby they reaped enormous profits.

In the early years of the industry, after Edwin Drake drilled the nation's first oil well in Titusville, Pennsylvania (1859), hordes of small competitors rushed into the new business. It was not a costly business to enter at that point, and soon numerous firms were competing intensely. Prices and the supply of crude oil and its refined forms fluctuated wildly. Three refining centers quickly arose—Pittsburgh, Philadelphia, and Cleveland—and from among the Ohio refiners came the man who eventually managed to organize the industry, John Davison Rockefeller.

The future oil magnate started out in 1859 in the produce business and entered petroleum refining in 1863. From the very first, Rockefeller showed a keen ability to choose able associates, and he became the nucleus of a talented group of financial and managerial partners. The Standard Oil Company was founded in 1867. (Its business was in kerosene, what was called illuminating oil, as the development and widespread use of the gasoline-powered automobile was still decades away.) By 1870 the firm had two large, efficient refineries that together represented about one-tenth of the nation's refining capacity. Because his company was Cleveland's largest refiner, Rocke-feller was able to secure preferential rates from railroads anxious to haul his large, steady shipments. Thus began what would prove to be a pattern in which Rockefeller was able to whipsaw the railroads, exploiting their competitive weaknesses to his own advantage. He persuaded other Cleveland refiners to join with him to secure lower rates and better profits. Arguing that the other Cleveland firms could not compete with Standard's efficient refineries and its lower transportation rates, Rockefeller pressured them to sell out to him or face ruin. Early in the decade of the 1870s Standard Oil succeeded in dominating the petroleum business in the Cleveland region and then turned its attention to national developments.

Refiners all over the nation were growing unhappy with the continuing unsettled state of their industry. Manufacturers were turning out kerosene, lubricating oils, and other products in such volume that prevailing profits and prices seemed threatened by overcapacity. In order to improve their own economic position, refiners needed to achieve some degree of control over the production of crude oil, as well as its refining, transportation, and distribution. Their initial answer was an attempt at a trade association, the National Refiners' Association, begun in 1872 with Rockefeller as president. The association included representatives from the major refining areas (by now, Cleve-

land, Pittsburgh, New York, Philadelphia, and the crude oil regions in western Pennsylvania). Those representatives allocated
quotas for the production of crude and the sale of refined oil.
Some of the firms pumping crude oil quickly formed a similar
group to organize their end of the business. It soon became apparent, however, that their efforts were not working. Firms outside the associations refused to cooperate, and even the associations' own members sometimes broke the agreements in an
effort to get more than their allotted share of the business. The
organizations collapsed, doomed by their weak controls and
lack of enforcement powers.

Having tried loose alliances and found them wanting,
Rockefeller and his colleagues set out to build a single big company to control the industry. Using the old Cleveland strategy of
combining superior productive efficiency with rebates in transportation, Standard strengthened its position. Gradually, major
refiners around the nation were pressured or persuaded to sell
out to Standard. Because they received generous rewards for
their businesses in the form of stock in Standard Oil, and because they could have a voice in the committee-style management of the combination, refiners sold out in the belief that
profits could be assured by that company. These mergers were
often kept secret, and the various companies continued to operate under their old names. By the end of the 1870s, a great horizontal combination had been built; now the Standard Oil interests controlled about nine-tenths of the petroleum refining
capacity of the United States.

The giant horizontal amalgam, however, was an administrative and legal mess. Because the law generally forbade one corporation from owning stock in another and discouraged a firm
chartered in one state from owning property in another state,
Standard was put together with a patchwork of subterfuges.
Rockefeller and his compatriots personally held the stock of the
companies controlled by Standard Oil as trustees for their stockholders in an attempt to get around the law. By 1879 an informal version of the trust had been invented by Standard; a handful of trustees held the stock of out-of-state companies "in trust"

for Standard's stockholders. Early in 1882 a Trust Agreement formalized the arrangement, and trust certificates were exchanged for the stock of Standard Oil. This apparently legal detour around existing laws was imitated in the 1880s by various combinations, including the trusts in sugar and in distilling. Growing political pressure and the appearance of New Jersey's 1889 general incorporation law giving blanket permission for New Jersey corporations to hold stock in out-of-state corporations made the trust form shortlived. It was replaced by the holding company (after 1889) as the favored instrument for combination.

In the years after 1882, Standard Oil faced challenges from both foreign and domestic competitors, challenges that led it to move to consolidate its central control over the companies it owned. In 1884 the trust opened headquarters on Broadway, from which it directed the increasing integration and expansion of its oil empire. Most of Standard's market lay overseas, and the development of Russian oil by the powerful Nobel interests prompted Standard to close inefficient refineries and relocate refining operations in areas closer to water transportation to cut costs and rebuff the threat from Europe. The discovery of new oil fields in the United States and the continual appearance of independent refiners led Rockefeller's company to integrate backward into the production of crude oil and forward into transportation and marketing. The creation of networks of pipelines to move both crude and refined oil was especially critical to Standard's maintenance of it leading position. Utilizing its efficiency, its financial strength, new technologies, and the harsh competitive techniques associated with its name—the use of rebates, intimidation, an espionage network reporting on uncooperative businesses, and ruthless vengeance for troublemakers—Standard built by the early 1890s a vast, vertically integrated company involved in every aspect of the petroleum business. Standard's near-monopoly position did nevertheless decline thereafter with the rise of competitors such as Gulf and Texaco in the new oil fields of the Southwest around the turn of the century. The Supreme Court's 1911 dissolution of Standard into a number of firms later completed the oil industry's transition into a business dominated by a few firms rather than by a single company.

Manufacturers in other industries learned with interest of the innovations of Standard Oil, and soon additional producers were trying to imitate its success in achieving control, stability, and handsome profits. Participants in the sugar refining industry were definitely interested, for their business was remarkably similar to oil refining. In the years shortly before the Civil War, major technological improvements in sugar refining, in the words of Alfred Eichner (*The Emergence of Oligopoly: Sugar Refining as a Case Study,* 1969), "had, in effect, created an entirely new industry." Those advances made it possible to mass produce sugar of uniform quality in large refineries for the first time. A number of new firms arose, built large refineries with the latest technology in East Coast cities, and successfully competed with the older Louisiana sugar companies. The period of the Civil War and the years immediately following it constituted good times for the manufacturers supplying the demand of urban areas in the eastern United States. During that initial period of growth, producers made "high profits" that attracted new firms and encouraged existing manufacturers to expand, according to Eichner's study.

By the 1870s, however, the industry ran into the troubles that afflicted some others in the same period—instability, falling prices, and declining profit rates due to the potential of the supply being greater than the demand. As the initial period of growth and high profits gave way to the price wars of the 1870s and early 1880s, the refiners' profit margin grew thinner and thinner. Because the industry was one that required large fixed investments, most firms were "no longer able to cover their full costs, if an adequate return on invested capital is included as part of their costs," Eichner reported. Investment in a sugar refinery was "sunk" into the plant and was difficult to liquidate or transfer to other uses, so even marginal producers stayed in the business, adding to the problem of overproduction. Sugar refiners, like other manufacturers, soon turned to associations or

pools in an attempt to regulate output and prices and thus
restore high profits. The first counterpart to oil's National Refiners' Association was inaugurated in sugar in 1880. Despite
elaborate pooling arrangements, these efforts soon collapsed,
and for the usual reasons. Other attempts at cooperation followed, but they also failed. As a result, producers began to look
toward combination.

After difficult negotiations, most of the big refiners reached
agreement to form a horizontal combination, using the legal device Standard Oil had pioneered—the trust. In 1887 eighteen
refiners joined secretly and promulgated a trust agreement, exchanging the stock of their individual enterprises for the trust
certificates. As in the case of the oil mergers, the producers who
agreed to join were offered attractive prices for their businesses.
Soon the sugar trust found itself exercising more and more central direction over the (initially) highly autonomous subdivisions, ordering the closing of older, less efficient plants to cut
costs and raise profits. In 1891 the company took advantage of
the New Jersey incorporation law and reorganized itself as
American Sugar Refining, a *corporation* rather than a trust.

In subsequent years, however, the sugar combine found it
ever more difficult to maintain its early near-monopoly position.
A new raw material source—sugar beets—arose to compete
with sugar cane, and the company expended enormous funds to
counter that threat in the 1890s. In addition, it proved impossible to keep all competitors out, despite the unsavory methods
of competition of American Sugar Refining. These practices included railroad rebates (by then definitely illegal) and attempts
to strong-arm wholesalers into refusing to handle the products
of any other sugar company. Such ruthless competition, coupled
with the firm's traditional secrecy and the refusal of company
officials to cooperate with governmental inquiries, gave the
combination a bad reputation. Eventually this led to an (unsuccessful) antitrust suit. Nevertheless, sugar refining had by the
early 1900s evolved into an industry dominated by a few large
firms and not by one. As other businesses later discovered, it often proved quite possible to influence the course of prices when

the industry was composed of a relatively few big producers, when the dominant firm set a price and others followed. This was known as "price leadership." The creation of the sugar combination and the subsequent success of sugar refiners in restoring higher profits added further luster to the appeal of horizontal combinations in the eyes of other manufacturers.

The rise of the third of the major corporations we will look at in some detail—American Tobacco—revealed a pattern strikingly similar to that of oil and sugar refining. American Tobacco appeared in the cigarette industry, a relatively new business (like petroleum and refined sugar). The industry arose after the Civil War and experienced a very high growth rate throughout the 1870s and the first half of the 1880s. During that period, profits were good and producers were happy. By about the mid-1880s, however, demand was leveling off, and the industry entered a period of stringent competition brought on by overcapacity. With the invention of the Bonsack cigarette-rolling machine and its introduction by James B. Duke in the mid-1880s the existing production system of hand rolling became obsolete. Mechanization of the production process immediately expanded the potential supply to great heights.

Once demand leveled off and overcapacity set in, the producers fell to intensive competition. They used heavy advertising as a competitive weapon, and by the end of the eighties, advertising costs devoured approximately 20 percent of the companies' incomes. The manufacturers soon tired of this strenuous competition and began to search for a way to stabilize profits.

A few weak efforts at controlling output and prices followed, but with little result. During the discussions among the major producers about how to resolve the problem of overcapacity and costly competition, the alternative of a cartel with pooling arrangements was considered but rejected as too feeble a form of cooperation to get the job done. The earlier experiments with such arrangements in the railroads, and in the oil, sugar, and other industries, had clearly given such methods of seeking control a bad reputation in the business community. Ac-

cordingly, the cigarette producers decided after months of negotiations to create a horizontal combination.

The American Tobacco Company was founded in 1890, the
first major combination formed as a holding company under
New Jersey's freshly passed general incorporation statute. As
did so many other combinations, American Tobacco at first operated with highly independent subdivisions, but its managers
soon were centralizing control from the Manhattan headquarters
and moving toward vertical integration. During the next ten or
twelve years, the cigarette combination extended its influence
into other branches of the tobacco manufacturing industry. Utilizing strong-arm competitive methods such as selective price
wars (with what were called "fighting brands"), coercive agreements with jobbers to force them to handle only American
Tobacco's goods, as well as the weapon of massive advertising
to swamp competitors, the tobacco combine achieved control
over the manufacture of smoking tobacco, chewing tobacco,
and snuff in addition to its control of cigarettes. If ever there
was what most people would think of as a "bad trust," it was
American Tobacco. The federal government prosecuted the firm
under the Sherman Act in 1907, and the Supreme Court in 1911
upheld its conviction, ordering that it be broken up into several
companies. Even the smaller firms created by the dissolution of
the industry giant were each of substantial size, however, and
oligopoly proved to be almost as profitable and stable as the
near-monopoly that American Tobacco had attempted to maintain. The efforts by manufacturers to control prices and avoid
competition had ultimately led to a highly concentrated industry
dominated by a few large firms—the pattern common among
numerous industries after the rise of big business.

The motivation of the individuals who formed these horizontal combinations was somewhat different from that of those,
such as Swift and Singer, whose giant businesses were created
through vertical growth and marketing innovations. Here the
primary goal was simply to gain control over an industry in order to influence output, prices, and profits. Other purposes were
involved, of course, such as securing economies of scale and re-

ducing costs, but the overriding objective was improved control over output and prices. (Even so positive an analyst of big businesses as Alfred Chandler wrote in a 1984 *Business History Review* essay that "for most American enterprises the motivation for the initial incorporation as a holding company was to control competition.") If that goal could be reached and maintained over the long run, monopoly profits could be won, which would be a burden to society. These early horizontal combinations provoked a troubling question, one that was to grow more pressing as businesses in other industries attempted to follow the lead of Standard Oil, American Sugar Refining, and American Tobacco: could market forces or political intervention assure that the social benefits of such combinations would equal or outweigh the costs? The economy was on the brink of a tidal wave of combinations that would make that question more urgent than ever.

The Great Merger Wave

By the mid 1890s the appearance and notoriety of various horizontal combinations in the form of trusts or holding companies had helped prepare the way for the rapid proliferation of such businesses. Once a few successful and widely publicized combinations had gotten underway, leading business figures began to consider the possibility and the desirability of duplicating in their own industries the pattern of Standard Oil, American Sugar Refining, and American Tobacco. In any sort of sudden, massive alteration in the organization of many businesses, the force of example is strong, and the new forms are "in the air" or faddish.

A number of critical factors explain why the nation's industries began merging in huge numbers just around the turn of the century. Changes in the legal environment seem to have played a contributing role in readying the economy for the rapid spread of horizontal mergers. One important development was the appearance of state general incorporation laws (such as New Jersey's in 1889) that allowed one corporation to hold stock in others without having received special permission from the often politically hostile state legislatures. That change made it much easier to create holding companies and fold together the stock of different enterprises. The new general incorporation laws, designed to attract industry to—or at least encourage incorporation and its associated fees as revenues for—such states as New Jersey and Delaware, meant that a company could obtain a charter simply by filling out a form and paying a fee. The new company could then operate in and acquire subsidiaries in other states with less difficulty. These legal changes facilitated the rapid spread of mergers, as Donald Dewey argued in his *Monopoly in Economics and Law* (1959).

The law underwent many shifts in relation to business before the Sherman Antitrust Act of 1890, but the courts' interpretation of that act was central to the rise of big business. One of the interesting things about human activities is the extent to which carefully laid plans produce unintended consequences, and the political opposition to the spread of big business was such an instance. Congress had responded to public pressure to "do something" about the problem of concentration in the economy by passing the Sherman Act. The act was vague, simply outlawing "every . . . combination . . . in restraint of trade." The intent of the law and that of most of its supporters was to slow or halt the spread of big businesses and collusive practices, and to reassure those worried about the nation's course by encouraging a return to a more competitive economy of smaller firms. The particular way in which the courts interpreted the law, however, seemingly speeded up the appearance of the integrated corporation in the United States. This was so because the courts ruled that forms of cartel-like behavior were illegal under the act, but that unified combinations were in most instances acceptable. That is, the law forbade collusion by independent firms but did not necessarily outlaw the activities of integrated holding companies created by the legal union of previously separate businesses. The result was that independent businesses were led from cartel-like arrangements to combinations in part by the legal changes originally designed to prevent the rise of more big businesses.

As William Letwin's *Law and Economic Policy: The Evolution of the Sherman Antitrust Act* (1967) showed, the legal thickets surrounding the place of cartel behavior and horizontal combinations in American law both before and after the Sherman Act were dark and dense indeed. It is clear, however, that American law treated such issues very differently than did the legal systems of other industrial nations. The American legal system inherited from English law a strong distaste for cartels. Although cartel behavior was increasingly tolerated in England by about the middle of the nineteenth century, it continued to be frowned upon in the United States. (Tony Freyer's 1992 book, *Regulating Big Business: Antitrust in Great Britain and America, 1880–1990,* traced the long swings in attitudes toward cartels and mergers in the two nations.) Furthermore, in continental European nations such as France and Germany, cartels abounded and were quite legal. Agreements reached by European cartels could, therefore, be enforced in the courts, so they worked more satisfactorily there than did their counterparts in America. This was one reason why small, family-dominated firms tended to survive longer in those countries than in the United States. Many examples of the giant corporation certainly arose in early-twentieth-century Europe, but it is clear that the United States proved a more fertile ground for the spread of big businesses, and the reasons had to do in part with the respective legal frameworks in which business operated.

As Hans B. Thorelli pointed out in his *The Federal Antitrust Policy* (1955), both federal and state law appeared to oppose collusive practices in restraint of trade. Because they were forbidden to engage in cartel behavior, and, more important, because such agreements lacked the force of contracts and could not be enforced in court, American businesses moved more quickly to the genuine formal amalgamation of previously independent companies.

The Congress placed a heavy burden on the courts when it elected to pass such general, vague legislation about concentration. The Supreme Court and lower federal courts struggled with the endless questions that arose about big business and the antitrust law. A price-fixing agreement was obviously illegal, but what were the justices to do when one company sold its assets to another? Were such sales illegal if they resulted in restraint or reduction of trade or competition? Was it a matter of degree? How should the effort to create a monopoly be defined? What exactly was a monopoly—100 percent of an industry? 75 percent? 50 percent? Or did that differ with the particular conditions in each industry? If a monopoly or a restraint of trade did exist, how could it be broken up or reversed? Who would organize the new arrangements, and how could they be monitored and evaluated? While the courts continued to wrestle with such conundrums, businesses continued to organize their combinations. If the courts meant to shear the cartel sheep and bypass the integrated-firm goats, it was clearly better to be a goat than a sheep, or at least to look like one. Like the changes in state general incorporation laws, the importance of the Sherman Act was to encourage still further the growing eagerness to try horizontal combinations.

Another development closely linked with unleashing the merger proliferation seems to have been important changes in the nation's investment markets. Advances in transportation, communications, and the appearance of highly productive new technologies had made the new, large-scale, integrated corporation a possibility. The behavior of prices, profits, and growth rates had started businesses on a long search for cooperative means of controlling their economic environment, and pools and trade associations had proved unsatisfactory. That search for order, as we have seen, began in some industries even before the Civil War, when the early trade associations were formed. Beginning with the Panic of 1873, the hard times of the 1870s caused businesses in many industries to join in that search. Throughout the 1870s and 1880s cooperative efforts among manufacturers became common, as they had earlier become on the railroads. Particularly after the late 1880s, changes in the legal setting encouraged and facilitated the transition to the unified firm, and the success of a few highly publicized horizontal combinations had led others in business to think of the possibility of creating similar organizations. Changes in the capital markets removed the last significant institutional barrier and made it much easier to achieve cooperative solutions to competitive problems through mergers. Naomi Lamoreaux's *The Great Merger Movement in American Business, 1895–1904* (1985) argued that the onset of the severe depression that began with the Panic of 1893 provided the impetus that triggered the tidal wave of mergers at the end of the century. The economic troubles of many manufacturers in that depression led them to seek, as some had been doing for decades, a way out. The resulting rush to mergers both hastened and was hastened by the significant changes in the financial markets.

Before the early 1890s, there was virtually no national market for industrial securities. Except in the case of a few companies, it was not possible for potential investors to buy stock of an industrial firm as they so commonly do now. Railroad stocks and bonds accounted for almost all the securities of private businesses available to people in an open market. Industrial stocks were generally considered too risky for this sort of investment, though there was some small-scale trading of industrial shares (such as those of textile companies) on local markets before 1890. There was, however, no national market for "industrials," as they were called. As a result, owners of manufacturing businesses found their capital sunk in their firms and had little opportunity to liquidate their ownership if they wanted to. For example, if a steel-mill owner had a quarter-interest in a steel business and wanted to retire from the competitive fray, it was almost impossible to liquidate that interest unless the other owners or a very wealthy outsider wished to buy the quarter-interest. Under those circumstances the owner seeking an exit from the business might possibly have to stay in the firm for lack of a buyer or else settle for less than the interest was really worth in order to cash in. If, on the other hand, the unhappy owner held 25,000 of the 100,000 shares in a business and there was a large, well-established trade in industrial securities, all or part of those shares could be sold much more easily and probably at a better price. Were such a securities market in place, a large number of people could bid for small blocks of the shares

and view them simply as investments and not as any real obliga-
tion to get into the steel business. Such a market would be a
much more accurate and efficient mechanism for evaluating the
worth of assets and turning them into cash. In the 1890s such a
market arose for the first time, as the securities of industrial corporations gained widespread acceptance among investors and
came to be listed on the New York Stock Exchange and traded
all over the nation and abroad. The creation of an industrial securities market also made it much easier to build large combinations, and the appearance of an increasing number of successful
big businesses helped explain the market for industrials.

The growing attempts to form horizontal combinations produced a ready demand for the funds available from investors in
the United States and Europe. By the end of the 1880s a small
number of the trust certificates of major horizontal combines
had begun to find a market, but only among very speculative investors. Conservative investors would not think of buying such
securities because they considered them too risky. By the early
1890s, however, this situation began to change.

During the first years of that decade, as Thomas Navin and
Marian Sears showed (*Business History Review,* June 1955),
some of the new, large, and apparently legal holding companies
began to issue preferred stock, sometimes with the aid of highly
reputable bankers. These securities, aided considerably by the
growing feeling that the holding companies were on sounder legal ground than the cartel-like trusts, found places on the
nation's most important stock exchanges. Many leading investment bankers, including the conservative and highly prestigious
J. P. Morgan, continued to regard the new industrials with some
misgivings, though Morgan himself did help finance one such
company—General Electric—in 1893. When the stock market
suffered a long downturn in the depression that began in that
same year, however, the industrials weathered the storm better
than the stocks of most railroads. By the time the economy
turned up again in a few years, bankers and investors had gained
considerable confidence in industrial securities. In addition, the
railroad sector, for decades almost the exclusive focus of trading

in stocks, had by the 1890s grown stale and tired. The great period of growth by then lay behind the railroads rather than ahead of them, and they had been plagued by financial problems and bankruptcies for years, a situation only worsened by the depression of the nineties. The capital markets were increasingly ready to receive large issues of securities from big businesses in manufacturing. When the most gilt-edged banking house of all, J. P. Morgan and Company, underwrote the creation of the Federal Steel Company in 1898, it became clear even to the most cautious of investors in the United States and Europe that the time had come to get in on a good thing. The fact that a solid, brisk market was appearing for industrial securities made it much easier for business leaders to create large combinations. It was considerably less difficult to talk independent manufacturers into giving up their companies to form part of a giant corporation if they knew they could always turn their shares into cash in the stock market. In addition, most bankers and promoters who helped work out the financial arrangements by which companies merged saw to it that the new combinations were capitalized at considerably more than the worth of their separate parts (a practice many people denounced as "watering" stock). This made it easier to woo reluctant manufacturers into joining a new combination by offering them shares that might bring more in the stock market than the manufacturers had thought their companies were worth. This suspicious situation was brought about by the fact that the amalgamating firms and promoters found stock-market investors ready to buy shares in the new businesses, even at prices considerably higher than the per-share net worth of the corporations. Investors believed in the future growth of the new companies and probably expected good dividends and even higher stock prices in the future. In many cases they got what they expected, but in many other cases the results were nothing short of grim. Then as today, the success of the investments varied greatly, depending on the particular company. In any event, the willingness of investors to pay high prices for stocks made it possible for the promoters and underwriters like Morgan to make enormous profits, and for the own-

ers of previously independent concerns to get more than they
might have imagined when they joined a combination. The result was that the owners of autonomous businesses found combination increasingly attractive.

Naomi Lamoreaux's *Great Merger Movement* emphasized
not only the influence of the depression of the 1890s in height-
ening price competition and thus encouraging mergers, but also
pointed out that particular kinds of industries were especially
prone to amalgamation. "Capital-intensive, mass-production
industries in which . . . expansion had been rapid on the eve
of the Panic of 1893"—industries dominated by relatively new
firms—these were the most likely ones to seek relief through
merger.

During the decade after 1895, the great merger movement
flourished, and nothing like it was seen before or since in the
history of the nation's economy. Approximately three hundred
separate firms disappeared into mergers each year during those
ten years. By 1910, many of the nation's most influential big
businesses had been created either through vertical or horizontal
growth, or a mixture of the two. Just a partial list of modern industrial giants already born by 1910 included: petroleum companies such as Standard Oil, Gulf, and Texaco; rubber producers such as U.S. Rubber and Goodyear; metals firms including
U.S. Steel, Bethlehem Steel, American Smelting and Refining,
Jones and Laughlin Steel, Anaconda Copper, Phelps-Dodge, International Nickel, and National Lead; the electrical manufacturers General Electric and Westinghouse; food processors such
as American Sugar, Nabisco, United Fruit, Swift & Company,
and Armour; as well as scores of others including American Tobacco, Du Pont, Pittsburgh Plate Glass, American Can, Allis-
Chalmers, International Harvester, Singer, and Eastman Kodak.
It is no exaggeration to say that the structure of the American
economy for decades to come had been reshaped by the end of
the first decade of the twentieth century.

In many branches of industry, producers tried to create
large-scale businesses. Some of these concerns, like those mentioned above, were successes. Many others were not, as Arthur
S. Dewing's *Corporate Promotions and Reorganizations* (1914)

showed. Some rose like mushrooms in the night and disap-
peared almost as quickly. Among the giants that might have
been but failed to achieve long-run success, one could list such
unfamiliar firms as National Starch, U.S. Leather, American
Glue, National Salt, National Cordage, Standard Rope & Twine,
United Button Company, American Wringer, American Grass
Twine, National Novelty, Consolidated Cotton Oil, American
Woodworking Machinery, U.S. Dyewood and Extract, Ameri-
can Soda Fountain, National Wallpaper, Mt. Vernon-Woodberry
Cotton Duck, among others.

An early, spectacular example of failure was National Cordage. Manufacturers of cordage (rope and twine) tried associations and pools in the 1870s and 1880s without effecting the stability and security they desired. In 1887 four of the leading
companies took the next step, uniting to form the National
Cordage Company. In an attempt to gain control of the industry,
the cordage combination embarked on an ambitious program of
expansion, acquiring additional mills that gave the company
nominal control of about 40 percent of the nation's rope and
twine production by 1890. In the summer of that year, the firm's
capital stock was increased tenfold to $15 million and still
more competitors were brought into the combine. By the early
months of 1892, the company effectively controlled approximately 90 percent of the cordage mills in the United States. It
moved to the forefront of the new industrial giants, enjoying the
backing of powerful New York bankers, and the financial press
hailed it as a sure success.

Within a single year, however, the mighty cordage trust was
on the rocks. Competitors sprang up on every hand and the
trust's control of the industry slipped badly. Its financial
troubles came to a head in the first week of May, 1893—the
firm was unable to pay its obligations, its securities plummeted,
and it went bankrupt with breathtaking speed. The nation's
leading financial journal summed up the events: "Cordage has
collapsed like a bursted meteor."

Another also-ran in the monopoly sweepstakes was the National Salt Company. That firm arose in the giddy days of the
great merger wave as a combination of salt producers in New

York State in 1899. By parlaying mergers and making imprudent financial arrangements with other producers, the promoters of National Salt secured by 1900 control of about 85 to 90 percent of the industry east of the Rockies, according to the company's president. The firm then raised the price of salt. For about a year and a half the plan worked well and profits rolled in. The salt trust's fortunes soon suffered a sharp downturn, however, when outsiders rushed into the industry to grab a share of the bonanza. The combine encountered growing difficulty in meeting its financial obligations under the arrangements made earlier to secure its control of the industry. During the course of those troubles, the company defaulted on payments due cooperating salt producers and then tried to escape its obligations by asking the courts to set aside the now troublesome agreements on the grounds that they represented a conspiracy in restraint of trade! The salt barons, it seems, were nothing if not flexible. Even their resourcefulness proved unequal to the task, though, and by 1902 the National Salt Company was in receivership.

Although concentration came to a great many industries, it did not "take" in all of them. Obviously, it was not enough merely to have the unscrupulous and greedy outlook attributed to the "robber barons." Riches were not simply lying on the ground for any would-be monopolists to pick up. What factors, then, underlay the ability of some businesses to last while others were quickly cut down and still others disappeared in the wake of later challenges?

A look at the history of concentration in industry in the twentieth-century American economy shows that, in general, the degree of overall concentration and its basic patterns were relatively stable for some time after 1910. To be sure, many circumstances and factors influenced whether a particular firm would become and remain a giant enterprise, including the quality of its management, timing, and luck. But the most important factors in accounting for the rise and persistence of a giant firm was its ability to employ new technology effectively to achieve and sustain genuine economies of scale and then link mass production to mass distribution. The difficulty and enormous expense of creating new, competitive firms in such industries as steel, nonferrous metals, petroleum, automobiles, rubber, machinery, electrical manufactures, and chemicals both explains the reluctance of outside competitors to venture into those areas as well as the lack of success for those who did plunge in. The companies that had already grown big in such industries by the early twentieth century enjoyed a very long lead in terms of capital investment in production and distribution networks, managerial talent, scientific or technological expertise (including advantageous patents), relationships with customers, and established market positions. Others found it very difficult (though not impossible) to enter and compete successfully with the existing giants. In some industries that involved little in the way of advanced technology, big businesses successfully discouraged competition through heavy advertising and the creation of powerful brand names. Makers of cigarettes and breakfast cereals, for example, raised the cost of introducing new products through massive advertising campaigns. Potential competitors were thus discouraged by the very high costs of advertising and of positioning goods in the retail markets, so the market share of the existing large firms was largely protected. In most low-technology industries, meanwhile, it was relatively inexpensive for new companies to enter the market, but still correspondingly difficult to maintain a high degree of concentration.

The combine in cordage, for example, was a poor gamble from the start. The producers could combine in order to gain control over prices, but they could not readily maintain that control. It was too easy for others, tempted by the high prices and profits, to enter the industry. The supply of raw materials was abundant, the cost of beginning production was low, and no control was possible at the marketing end of the business. When competitors appeared, the combination could buy them out for a time, but eventually it succumbed to the reestablishment of competition, which destabilized prices and sometimes brought the collapse of the combination. In many industries, then, the workings of market forces ensured that society would not be "held up" (at least not for very long) by horizontal combinations. Big business, it was clear, found richer soil in some industries than in others.

Even if the entrepreneur were in one of the industries that benefited from the rise of technologies that permitted economies of scale and that fit nicely into a vertically integrated set of economic activities, the possibility of failure still loomed. The patterns of success, however, seem reasonably clear, as detailed in the work of Alfred D. Chandler, Jr. In *Scale and Scope* (1990), he reviewed the history of giant enterprises in three of the world's leading industrial economies—the United States, Great Britain, and Germany. In all three nations, Chandler argued, in order to succeed, "entrepreneurs had to make three sets of interrelated investments." They not only had to invest in "production facilities large enough to exploit a technology's potential economies of scale or scope," but they also had to build far-flung marketing and distribution networks and recruit and hold an army of managers to administer them, to "monitor and coordinate" production and distribution and to "plan and allocate resources for future production and distribution." If they could do all that, and if they proved resourceful enough to react creatively to the threats and the opportunities constantly presented by the changing economic, social, and political environment, they could sustain their firms' places in the twentieth-century economy.

Some large firms did appear in low or middling technology, unintegrated industries, often through their success in creating name brands through advertising. In general, though, such sectors remained relatively unconcentrated. Examples of the latter included textiles, leather, printing and publishing, lumber and wood, furniture, clothing, most food products, and similar industries. Clearly, the potential empire-builder of the turn of the century would have done well to choose the right kind of industry in which to seek and hold the gains enjoyed by the major corporations that endured long after the great merger movement. For those entrepreneurs who did choose the right, technologically complex industries, short-term market constraints were weaker. There, society had cause for concern about the implications of the advent of large-scale corporations because their market power might permit monopoly profits.

The new big businesses called forth profound worries about the danger of corporate power in an emerging economic order that was fundamentally different from the old, classically competitive one. The old days of small firms and the kind of competition most economists still talk about—the "Golden Age of Competition," Alfred Eichner called it—were gone for decades to come in many important industries. In their search for stability, order, and steady profits, business leaders had eventually created large, integrated, unified firms that, along with a few similar companies, often formed concentrated or oligopolistic industries. These new businesses, unlike the older, smaller ones, seldom competed by offering prices appreciably lower than those of their major rivals. Price competition, they had learned, could be avoided by businesses that grew so big that their output formed a significant enough share of the market to influence the pricing of others. In the older economy, the number of producers was usually so large and the size of each business so small that one manufacturer could usually cut prices without affecting the output and price decisions of the many other firms in the same line. Such behavior under the new conditions of oligopoly and high fixed costs, however, often led to the long periods of falling prices that had first led businesses down the road to combination. Instead, much of the economy had moved into a new era of "administered" prices. Sometimes, as in the case of the steel industry, the largest firm would exercise price leadership. Under that system, the other big producers would simply follow the lead of the major company. Outright price-fixing through formal collusion became relatively rare, not only because it remained illegal, but also because it was no longer necessary. The major producers, now armed with improved cost accounting, knew their costs well, and they also had a pretty good idea of their competitors' costs. Therefore it was relatively easy to arrive at a sort of "standard" industry price which every player tacitly agreed to maintain and which greatly improved the chances for a good return on the capital invested in the enterprises.

Instead of competing on the basis of prices, the oligopolists learned to compete in other, less crude ways. These included different methods of sales promotion (mass-media advertising, in particular) and different quality or alleged quality in goods and services. The new competition meant constant striving for the most efficient systems of organization for production and distribution, and a never-ending effort to plan, react to changing circumstances, and allocate resources so as to keep the enterprise growing via new products and services. It was the large, complex corporation, rather than Adam Smith's classical and invisible market forces, that came to be the means through which modern economic life was ordered in many vital industries.

Later, those managing the corporations would figure out additional ways to protect or improve their share of the market, such as introducing concepts of planned obsolescence, the "latest style," and other mechanisms through which the psychological needs of consumers would be influenced and satisfied. In some cases, such as the automobile industry, the older ideas of products as utilitarian objects was replaced by the notion of products as symbols of status, sex appeal, and material achievement. Subtle (and sometimes not so subtle) appeals to pride, prejudice, fear, and the endless varieties of human desire often replaced the older, nineteenth-century appeals to what consumers wanted then (or were thought to want)—thrift, utility, and durability. Other barriers beyond those in marketing could sometimes be created, such as through the aggressive use of patents, to prevent competitors from developing troublesome competing technologies. The new forms of competition were part of a radically different economic and social environment.

As big businesses spread through many industries at the center of the American economy near the end of the nineteenth century, it appeared that a brave new world had emerged. Oligopolies, barriers to entry, administered prices, competition on grounds other than price, and vast concentrations of wealth and power in private hands now ruled in many sectors. A great many Americans wondered whether the nation was better or worse off.

Top: Before big business: A world of water-borne entrepreneurial firms and merchant dominance in New York City.
New York Public Library. NYPG91-F178 003F.
Bottom: Cincinnati waterfront 1848. From the collection of The Public Library of Cincinnati and Hamilton County

Women found opportunities for participation in the paid labor force in the early textile mills. North Wind Picture Archives.

Left: Industrialist John Davison Rockefeller. National Portrait Gallery, Smithsonian Institution.
Right. Financier John Pierpont Morgan. Gift of H. S. Morgan, National Portrait Gallery, Smithsonian Institution.

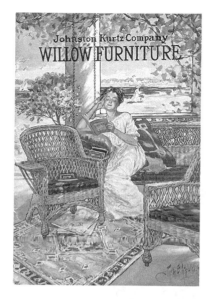

Left: Advertisers depicted the pleasures of a consumer society. Johnson-Kurtz Company Willow, 1911 catalog cover, University of Delaware Library, Newark DE.
Below: Bending fenders at Overland Factory, 1909. Courtesy of the Detroit Public Library, National Automotive History Collection.

EDGAR THOMSON WORKS 1875

Top: Carnegie's Edgar Thomson Steel Works, 1875. Library and Archives Division, Historical Society of Western Pennsylvania, Pittsburgh, PA.
Bottom: Ford factory, first moving assembly line, 1913. Library of Congresss, #16238. Courtesy of the Francis Loeb Library. Harvard Design School.

In 1908, in lower Manhattan, the Singer Company completed its signature building, then the world's tallest structure. Library of Congresss, #19875, Courtesy of the Francis Loeb Library. Harvard Design School.

These views show
elements of the
enormous Sears
Roebuck complex in
Chicago, 1910. More
than 9,000 employees
took orders, shipped
goods, and handled
more than 100,000
shipping tickets as well
as thousands of dollars
in cash and more than
33,000 money orders
and checks every nine-
hour workday.
Opposite top: Socializ-
ing in the women's
cafeteria.
Middle: Sears
distribution center
located on Chicago's
railroad yards.
Bottom: Closing hour,
5:30–6:00 p.m. on
Harvard Street.
Top right: This engine
house provided all the
power, heat, and light
for the entire Sears
complex. It occupied
30,000 square feet of
space
Bottom right: The Sears
long-distance switch-
board serviced 20
trunk lines, employed 4
operators and had 135
telephones installed.
Photographs courtesy
www.Chicagology.com.

In 1904, the mass-marketers at the Larkin Company opened a new headquarters in Buffalo, New York, designed by Frank Lloyd Wright. Buffalo & Erie County Historical Society.

Top: Homestead Steel Works, 1907. Hagley Museum and Library. *Bottom: J. P. Morgan & Co., Wall Street, New York City.* Library of Congress, LC-G612-T-51733 DLC.

Metropolitan Life was one of the large businesses that employed women in clerical posts. Its 50-story headquarters is shown here under construction, ca. 1908. New York Public Library. NYPG91-F204 026F.

A 125-ton steam hammer (shown with man for scale) made by Bethlehem Iron Company, 1891. Courtesy of the American Iron and Steel Institute (AISI).

Top: Great wealth was displayed through palatial homes, such as steel magnate Charles Schwab's in New York City. Library of Congress, #LC-D4-73037 DLC.
Bottom: Marshall Field & Co. department store, Chicago, Ill., c. 1907. Library of Congress, #LC-D4-34698.

Offices rose in the sky in the era of big business. Flat-Iron Building, designed by Daniel Burnham, Fifth Avenue and Broadway, New York, c. 1902. Library of Congress, #LC-D4-18842.

CHAPTER THREE

Corporate Triumph: "Capitalistic, Centralizing, and Mechanical"

During any period of rapid, widespread upheaval in society, people undergo enormous stress and tension as the old ways yield to the new. Sometimes the resulting shifts in power and opinion even touch off violent, radical reactions. Most often, however, society simply gropes its way to a gradual acceptance of change, and a new brand of social equilibrium emerges. The rise of big business and the triumph of industrial civilization certainly constituted a massive social change during the years bracketed by the Civil War and World War I. The upheaval was great, and for many the acceptance of the rising corporate order was painful indeed. "Such great revolutions," Henry Adams noted in his autobiography in 1905, "commonly leave some bitterness behind." As the twentieth century began to unfold, however, it gradually became clear that not only was big business here to stay; it was here to conquer almost all before it. The giant corporation proved to be the seedbed of a new social and economic order. The new managerial class, governed by the engineering values of efficiency and systematic approaches to problems, having first arisen to create and then to serve the corporation, soon became the dominant element in an urban and then suburban civilization. Other segments of the great middle class quickly found in big business a complex and comprehensive set of organizing values; soon almost the entire society would fall under the influence of corporate ways of doing things. This did not happen universally or instantly, to be sure, but the corporation established its hegemony with relative speed and became the dominant institution in American society.

The triumph of the corporation as the most powerful element in American life worked on many levels, affecting politics most immediately, reinforcing the prevailing gender, class, and ethnic order of American society, reshaping labor, and signaling the enshrinement of technology and science as the new American gods and consumption as a way of life. In short order the corporation would restructure much of society according to its own image. Most of those developments, however, would become wholly clear only with the passage of time. As the nineteenth century drew to a close, the issues seemed very much in doubt.

Uncertainty and unease about the emerging order of corporations and "trusts" took many forms. Workers felt increasingly helpless when confronting giant corporations. Struggling in a hostile legal and political environment, they tried to fight back by forming unions and staging work stoppages. The decades following the Civil War were marked by extraordinary levels of labor-management conflict, often punctuated by violence. Many of the most widespread and bloodiest strikes involved big businesses, such as the railroads, the Pullman company, and the giant iron and steelmakers. So disruptive were the conflicts between labor and business that many in the middle class came to feel that the "labor problem" was the principal threat to the nation's peace and stability. And, in a nation that was still predominantly agrarian, the deep concerns on the nation's farms made big business an issue of continental scale. Farmers found themselves increasingly subject to the fluctuations of a national and often international market for their produce, a set of complex economic factors they did not always understand. Although most recent analyses have found few hard facts to justify farmers' economic complaints, they nevertheless reacted with fear and loathing as they realized how fully commercialized American agriculture had become—and how fully they lay at the mercy of market forces. The nation was moving away from the older world of independent producers living in island communities and toward a society based on organization and consumption. When their fears mounted, agrarians tended to blame their woes on the murky dealings of railroad executives, eastern bankers, industrialists, crooked politicians, grain merchants, and other sinister individuals.

Agrarian protest began shortly after the close of the Civil War with the formation of the Patrons of Husbandry, better known to history as the Grangers. They were soon supplanted by agrarian political pressure organizations called farmers' alliances, whose successes in electing candidates to state and federal offices in the 1880s led them to form a national ("third") party in 1892. Joining with dissident workers and with other groups, the farmers spawned the Populist Party, declaring in their famous Omaha platform of 1892 that "a vast conspiracy against mankind" was underway and that a populist crusade would have to be waged to crush it.

During the last three decades of the nineteenth century, a varied array of protest groups voiced their unhappiness. A small minority of the nation's workers joined to create viable unions, first in the form of broad-gauged, reform-oriented ones such as the National Labor Union and the Knights of Labor. Those organizations tried to appeal to all segments of working people, and they sought to overturn the wage system and produce goods through cooperative enterprises. Eventually such groups merged with the populists in the 1890s. In addition to the farmers and workers who called for fundamental change, another reform impulse of the period focused on the rather confused fight to alter the currency. A succession of political parties and interest groups from the Greenbackers through the advocates of the increased issue of silver coinage all sought to solve society's problems through inflation. Others attacked different aspects of the national discontent. The followers of Henry George worked for a more nearly equal distribution of wealth through taxing privately owned land, which they believed to be the key to reversing the exploitation of the people. Many of these reform groups coalesced in the 1890s in the Populist Party and (in 1896) gained control of the national Democratic Party. They then sought to concentrate their efforts on the silver issue in the famous contest for the presidency between their candidate, William Jennings Bryan, and Republican William McKinley. In hindsight, this was in many respects a cultural rear-guard action, a last stand against the emerging America that was more centralized, more corporate, and more governed by the values of materialism and consumption than ever before. Bryan's crushing defeat in that election demoralized the agrarian crusade, and that fact, perhaps along with the return of prosperity to the farm belt, resulted in the retreat of most farmers from the reform cause. Following the prescription of Kansas populist Mary Ellen Lease, they had raised less corn and more hell, but only until the price of corn rose.

The progressive movement then took up the cause, continuing to criticize railroads, giant manufacturing concerns, and influential bankers. The progressives mixed efforts to improve the democratic process (via secret ballots, direct election of Senators, the use of city managers rather than elected mayors, and so on) with attempts to control or attack businesses, as well as with some changes that the representatives of big business also favored, such as the creation of the Federal Reserve System in banking. Theodore Roosevelt gained a reputation as a "trust buster" by having his Justice Department prosecute several widely hated corporations, and Woodrow Wilson, running largely as an opponent of big business, won the White House in 1912. Unlike the populists, however, most progressives sensed that they could not turn back the clock, that it made more sense to try to discipline the new order of business organization than to try to destroy it.

The reform movements have all been chronicled and analyzed well by generations of historians, and there is little point in recounting the story here. For our purposes, however, we may overlook the intricacies of the historical treatment of the politics and motivations of the reform movements and look instead at some of the basic political and economic issues raised by the coming of big business. We will also touch briefly on some of the multiple meanings of the rise of the modern corporation for American life outside the explicitly political realm.

Perhaps the broadest, most diffuse issue that troubled Americans during the sixty years or so discussed in this book was the fear that the new economic order was destroying America's status as a land of opportunity; citizens in many walks of life found the revolution in business disturbing and worrisome for that reason. An ever-smaller percentage of the population seemed likely to find a living through the small businesses that were the nation's independent, family farms. Other persons who enlisted in the fight against big business included those whose jobs or social standing had been affected adversely, such as the wholesalers who found giant corporations taking over the marketing of more and more goods in the changing economy. Those in small businesses driven into bankruptcy or forced to sell out to a combination voiced angry resentment. In short, the ranks of progressivism swelled with people who had thrived in the older economy but whose businesses or livelihoods suddenly had little or no place in the world of oligopolies and integrated firms. Much of the unhappiness of such people was rooted in their traditional vision of what America was supposed to be. The ideal of the opportunity for all citizens to acquire and operate their own businesses, farms, or workshops died hard. The fascination with the goal of making "each man his own boss" extended throughout much of American society. This ideal never disappeared completely, and small businesses continued to characterize many sectors of the economy. As big business expanded its dominion over much of the economy, however, an increasing number of people came to realize that they would have to sacrifice the hope of going into business for themselves and accept the idea of going to work for an organization run by others. Most would accept it in time, and many would even come to see virtue in the idea of moving up within the world of organizations, but for millions of Americans it was a bitter pill.

Critics of big business cited some of these basic attitudes when they testified before the U.S. Industrial Commission, a turn-of-the-century governmental body set up to investigate the problem of growing concentration in industry. Mr. P. E. Dowe, the representative of an association of traveling salesmen (a group hard hit by corporate integration into marketing), voiced the American Dream of the Gilded Age: "Every commercial traveler hopes to attain, both as the goal of the ambitious and progressive businessman and as an equitable return for years of hard work under trying conditions, a business of his own or in conjunction with others." Recalling the traveling men who had been forced to go to work for huge combinations and thus give up their independence, Dowe noted the passing of the old order and conjured up a bleak vision of the future. "The history of this country," he declared, "gives examples of poor boys who became great men, beginning at splitting rails, tanning hides, driving canal horses, etc., and we all know personally some illustration of self-made men; we have listened to the stories of father and grandsire, telling the younger generation of early struggles, and many instances have been cited where a few hundred or a few thousand dollars started them upon a career to fame and fortune. Trusts have come, however, as a curse for this generation and a barrier to individual enterprise. What will be the prospects for our children? God-Almighty alone knows."

This fear of the effects of big business upon individualism, independence, and the cherished prospect of people to achieve upward mobility lay at the heart of the widespread unease about the emergence of the corporate world. Like the so-called "closing of the frontier" announced in the 1890s by historian Frederick Jackson Turner, the coming of giant corporations seemed to signal the end of an open, promising America and the beginning of a land of diminished opportunity. Many Americans who grew up on the philosophy of Ben Franklin and the dream of the self-made man were troubled by the new visions of success embodied in climbing corporate ladders and moving up organization charts.

Another disturbing aspect of the rise of big business was the ruthless and unscrupulous use of economic power by men like John D. Rockefeller and James B. Duke in order to crush their rivals. People objected to such unfair competitive practices as allowing secret rebates, waging selective price wars designed to drive competitors into bankruptcy and forcing them to sell out at bargain prices, refusing to supply wholesalers unless they agreed to market only the supplier's products, and the like. Critics of business lambasted these practices, and it is clear that most Americans agreed then and still agree that such behavior is predatory, unethical, antisocial, and a misuse of economic power. Initially, the nation tried to solve this difficulty by passing laws that specifically forbade the use of particular economic tactics. The railroad regulatory laws, for example, made illegal the use of rebates and different rates for the same classes of shippers. In manufacturing, the issue of unfair competitive practices primarily involved discriminatory behavior. A firm large enough to constitute a significant portion of an industry used the power inherent in its size to secure favorable treatment in the purchase of raw materials, in the transportation of goods, raw materials, or personnel, or in the marketing of products. Often the favorable treatment was justified because it was economically and socially advantageous (that is, it reflected genuine savings in bulk buying, transport, and mass merchandising), but sometimes it was not (as in the case of the rebates demanded by big shippers and denied to others making similar but less frequent shipments). Whenever other competitors could not secure equal treatment for equivalent business activities, unfair advantages accrued to the largest firms.

In time, however, it became clear that the nation's lawmakers could not outlaw specific practices as fast as inventive businesses could come up with new ones. As a result, it became the national policy to create regulatory agencies with broad general powers to oversee and discipline the competitive behavior of big businesses. Under the administration of Theodore Roosevelt, the U.S. Bureau of Corporations was set up as an agency to investigate and publicize the unethical competitive methods of offending businesses. The notion that publicity about the doings of big business would cause it to behave better was as old as the problem of big business itself and had been at the heart of the first wave of state railroad regulatory bodies, the "sunshine commissions." It quickly became apparent that this idea was too optimistic, and Roosevelt soon proposed a stronger regulatory body. In 1914, this body came into being in the form of the Federal Trade Commission, an agency armed with limited enforcement powers as well as with the right to investigate and publicize business activity. As it had done earlier with the railroads, the federal government tried to ensure acceptably fair business behavior by creating a regulatory commission to oversee and police the activities of private firms, but not to determine some definite degree of concentration in industry or engage in genuine planning. The evolution of the antitrust laws came to mean much the same thing. In its landmark 1911 decision in the Standard Oil case, the Supreme Court announced the so-called "rule of reason," which made a distinction between *good* and *bad* trusts, though the justices did not use those terms. Giant companies that operated reasonably fairly and did not use objectionable competitive methods, the high court indicated, would not be judged guilty of violating the antitrust legislation. The judiciary would not attack any firm on the basis of its size alone, but rather on the basis of its behavior.

The result of those developments was the creation of a new role for the national government in the economy as watchdog of the private sector, basically a negative, policing role. The combined efforts of the regulatory agencies, the Justice Department, and the courts were supposed to prevent the worst sorts of discriminatory use of economic power. In time, as Thomas K. McCraw's *Prophets of Regulation* (1984) made clear, regulation would take many, sometimes contradictory, forms, some aimed merely at disclosure and publicity, some opposed to monopoly, and still others having the effect of protecting and cartelizing powerful interests. The beginnings of regulation did clearly demonstrate that, in the face of the rise of giant corporations, the nation had made the political decision that the affairs of businesses (previously largely private) were subject to public scrutiny. The competitive behavior of business would therefore permanently become a legitimate concern of government. In essence, regulation became, as McCraw concluded, an ever-changing series of political settlements "undertaken in an effort to keep peace within the polity." It made as much sense as such settlements customarily do, and it represented a compromise, a painful acceptance of the corporate world.

Most Americans had come in the end to believe that big business was inevitable, that the new world of complex organizations, bureaucracy, and giant enterprise had permanently transformed their civilization. Some critics would continue to argue, as Woodrow Wilson did in the 1912 presidential campaign, that if only firms could be made to give up their unfair practices, much of the old system of smaller, more competitive companies would reemerge. The immoral, underhanded doings of the robber barons, this theory held, had prevented the normal workings of the competitive marketplace. Conspiracy and greed, many would prefer to believe, explained the rise of large-scale enterprises. As we have seen, however, relatively few companies owed their power primarily to the use of such tactics. The dynamics of industrial capitalism rested on much deeper and more substantial foundations. It surely was true that Andrew Carnegie, John D. Rockefeller, James Duke, and other "robber barons" were hard men—unyielding, ruthless, and willing to utilize every bit of economic muscle at their command to protect and enlarge their empires. The economic power they used so coldly, however, was usually based on their ability to marshal resources effectively on a huge scale, to create new goods and services, and to produce and distribute them more efficiently and cheaply than could much smaller companies. Rockefeller's dominion over oil ultimately rested on the fact that his costs were the lowest in the industry. The long-term success of Carnegie Steel was similarly based on its greater efficiency in production and distribution, not just on enormous greed or greater ruthlessness. Society could tell such business leaders to stop using rebates or other forms of arm-twisting, and the message could be strong enough to lessen their control or influence somewhat, but it could never be strong enough to restore the fabled "Golden Age of Competition." Bigness, in short, would not go away once unfair methods of competition were restrained. What then? Was the government to tear down Carnegie's mills and Rockefeller's refineries? Were federal or state planners to be given the power to control investment and pricing decisions throughout industry? Although the Interstate Commerce Commission played something of that role in transportation, it proved very difficult to push such powerful government oversight beyond the bounds of the "natural monopolies" in transportation or public utilities. The notion of centralized planning had little appeal to serious people witnessing their nation's emergence as the world's leading industrial nation. Instead, throughout society, the triumph of the corporation and its ways began to reshape modern America. In the political sphere, as we have seen, big business would be accepted and the polity would put in place its own versions of the corporation's bureaucracies, rules, systems, managers, engineers, and lawyers.

Although the new corporations now did much of the coordinating and planning that had earlier rested in the invisible hand of the market, the power of the market remained great. Competition repeatedly reasserted itself in the long run, even in industries dominated by only a handful of firms that no longer competed primarily based on price. Excess profits could undoubtedly be won for a time through market power, but this eventually invited new entrants, just as it always had. The new economy certainly did not meet the economist's ideal standard of perfect competition, and sometimes it took longer than critics wanted for competitive forces to emerge. But the behavior of the large firms in the center economy generally proved to be reasonably competitive, most of the time, in the long run.

Even when measured by the economist's theoretical standards of perfect competition, it is not wholly clear that the nation was entirely worse off after the coming of big business and the appearance of more concentrated industries. In the earlier era, local monopolies had often flourished behind the barrier of higher transportation costs. As economists Stanley Engerman and Kenneth Sokoloff wrote, "the expansion in the size of markets and in the size of firms" meant "alternative sources of supply" as a result of "lowered transportation costs and increased competition in many markets." This, they concluded, "may have meant a gain to consumers relative to the earlier situation of local monopolies."

Engerman and Sokoloff further noted that the pioneers in big business in manufacturing in the 1880s "tended to be of the vertical type, based upon the desire to link the production and distribution of output, the advantages in obtaining supplies within a merged firm, and also to deal more effectively with technological complexity." And, although "horizontal mergers led to increased concentration in many industries," they "were often unsuccessful . . . and did not persist for long time periods unless there were some efficiency or scale gains."

The large firm represented both a solution to many of the competitive problems that plagued business in the late nineteenth century and a means of organizing and managing the new technologies of the era. That era later came to be called the Second Industrial Revolution, and the corporation was customarily the vehicle through which it had its greatest impact. The giant new integrated firms certainly did not replace all other ways of doing business, nor did they signal an "end of history" in which change came to a halt because no more perfect form could be imagined. As circumstances shifted after the rise of big business, industries and firms would continue to evolve. But by the early years of the twentieth century, the large, integrated corporation had become the instrument of choice for organizing activity within many sectors of the economy. These changes dismayed those nostalgic for the old ways and even worried many who saw economic benefits in large organizations. Most of the nation's decision makers, however, saw more progress than threat in big business. The corporate order clearly was accepted by the time of the outbreak of World War I in 1914, and perhaps as early as the election of 1896.

The patrician Henry Adams, one of the most thoughtful Americans of his or any generation, summed it up well in *The*

Education of Henry Adams, written in 1905. "For a hundred years," he mused, "the American people had hesitated, vacillated, swayed forward and back, between two forces, one simply industrial, the other capitalistic, centralizing, and mechanical." The rejection of the populist crusade in 1896 was for Adams the decisive moment. After that, it was clear to him that "a capitalistic system had been adopted, and if it were to be run at all, it must be run by capital and by capitalistic methods; for nothing could surpass the nonsensity of trying to run so complex and so concentrated a machine by Southern and Western farmers in grotesque alliance with city day-laborers." "Once admitted that the machine must be efficient," he concluded in resignation, "society might dispute in what social interest it should be run, but in any case it must work concentration." It would bring concentration not only in the economic and political spheres but in other realms of American life as well.

One of those areas transformed by the coming of the corporate world was the relationship between labor and management. The triumph of the corporation also changed, though not so deeply, the nature of work itself. The rise of the factory system and industrialization, it must be remembered, came before the creation of modern, large-scale enterprises. It was the First Industrial Revolution that initially brought the sorts of technological advances associated with the greater use of machines in production and the growing division of labor. The spread of machines, the factory, and the breaking down of complex jobs all previously performed by one person into a series of simpler, more specialized, but more repetitive, boring, and unchallenging tasks, were all developments that preceded big business. (Adam Smith himself had rhapsodized about the productivity increases that could come from the division of labor in the famous pin-factory examples in *The Wealth of Nations,* issued the same year as the Declaration of Independence.) Capitalists had introduced the new technologies of the industrial revolution both to capture increases in productivity and to strengthen their hands against their powerful skilled workers. Mechanization of production almost always meant a loss of power and status among skilled workers, whose rare talents had given them real leverage against their employers and had always made them the heart of the nation's labor union movement.

The spread of the division of labor and of mechanization led to what many historians called "deskilling," or the building of production skills into machines and processes to undermine the reliance on skilled workers. In industry after industry in the nineteenth century, the proliferation of mechanization brought discontent among the existing workforce, resistance by the elite skilled workers, labor unrest, and strikes—some of them vio lent. The transformation of some skilled work into a more dehu- manizing experience, with workers subjected to boring, repeti- tive tasks, was a part of industrialization itself. The introduction of deskilling also brought the beginnings of a long struggle over who would control shop-floor working conditions, the skilled workers or the bosses. Each time there was a significant change in the production process, a new machine or a new arrangement of machines, rancorous questions arose about who would de- cide how work would be done, in what sequence, and on what schedule. These conflicts, along with tensions brought by wage cuts in economic downturns, led to many of the strikes and vio- lent confrontations that sometimes broke out in or near the in- dustrial workplace. The resistance of skilled workers, unions, strikes, and bloody confrontations were generally the exception rather than the rule in the overall history of labor in the United States, but any such incidents were highly visible and therefore troubling signs of the stresses associated with the changing na- ture of work in an industrialized society. And such confronta- tions added considerably, as we have seen, to the political con- flicts of the nineteenth century. They were a sharp reminder that technological and industrial progress carried real costs as well as benefits. Conflicts such as the destructive railroad strikes of 1877, the Haymarket riot, and the strikes at Homestead and at Pullman contributed strongly to the widespread sense of unease about the direction in which the nation seemed to be moving. The coming of big business substantially heightened those anxi- eties, though the transformation that the corporation brought to the nature of work involved changes in degree rather than changes in kind.

The machine, the factory, mass production, deskilling, and alienation were all plainly evident before the pioneering industrial corporations appeared, but the new technologies that propelled so many of the early big businesses did mean the extension and expansion of the changes that made workers feel like insignificant cogs in giant, impersonal wheels. A new scale, new complexity, and an extreme subdivision of labor were associated with many of the technologies of mass production, continuous processing, and integrated production and distribution systems in the industries that made and marketed such things as farm machinery, electrical manufactures, tobacco products, refined petroleum, metals, sewing machines, flour, sugar, telephones, chemicals, and, especially, automobiles. It was the automobile industry, most prominently the company that would dominate that industry in its early stages—the Ford Motor Company—that would in time come to stand for the worst in the dehumanization of work that began with the rise of the factory system. Henry Ford had introduced the car for the masses, the revolutionary Model T, in 1908. In 1910 he opened his huge plant in Highland Park, Michigan, the site that quickly came to symbolize for many the evils of unrestrained mass production. Within a few short years of its opening Highland Park had become the birthplace of and the showcase for full-blown assembly-line production. That technology, perhaps more than any other, illustrated the extent to which the worker had become little more than an appendage to an enormous and ominous mechanical system. (Such concerns would inspire Charlie Chaplin's classic film *Modern Times* [1936], a comedic indictment of mass production.) In many of the mass-production industries of the late nineteenth and early twentieth centuries, there was a relative shrinkage of both skilled and unskilled jobs. Instead, more workers fell into a category of people who could be quickly trained and readily replaced to toil in highly mechanized factories, refineries, processing plants, and distribution centers. More and more frequently, commentators spoke not of the skilled and the unskilled but of the "semiskilled." More troubling was the fact that they also spoke of the rise of the "machine-tenders." The long journey begun in Adam Smith's pin factory had led ultimately to Highland Park. For millions of Americans, work itself had become, in Henry Adams's phrase, "capitalistic, centralizing, and mechanical."

Although the nature of work was altered by the rise of big business, the coming of the corporation meant even more fundamental changes in the relationships between labor and management outside the realm of the shop floor. The factory system found its first implementation in the textile industry, but by the 1880s it had spread, as Carroll D. Wright noted in his 1883 essay for the tenth federal census of manufactures, to the making of "boots and shoes, of watches, musical instruments, clothing, agricultural implements, metallic goods generally, firearms, carriages and wagons, wooden goods, rubber goods, and even the slaughtering of hogs." Daniel M. Nelson, in *Managers and Workers: Origins of the New Factory System in the United States 1880–1920* (1975), characterized the factory as the foreman's empire. Although owners often visited their factories and sometimes took a hands-on posture, much of the real power rested with the foreman. "Hiring and firing, assignment to tasks, setting the pay rate (by day or by piece), determining who got laid off or told to stay overtime, and resolving disputes all lay in the foreman's domain," wrote David Montgomery in *The Fall of the House of Labor: The Workplace, the State, and American Labor Activism, 1865–1925* (1987). "A foreman could favor those he liked with day rates, generous piece rates, relatively easy or pleasant tasks, permission to miss work to tend sick children or visit aged parents, and early recall from seasonal shutdowns." In some highly skilled work environments, foremen were rare, and senior skilled craft workers handled decisions about shop-floor operations. In both situations, owners and what we would today think of as managers played a minor role in basic production decisions. Turnover was high, workers (especially the less skilled) moved frequently from place to place and job to job, periods of unemployment were common, the manufacturing labor force in general was relatively small, and the treatment of workers was, by later standards, harsh. The term often applied to work relations in this era—the *drive system*—says much about the climate on the job. There was virtually no job security and very little in the way of benefits beyond the day's or the week's wage. There was little notion of the "rights of labor." David Brody, in *Steelworkers in America: The Nonunion Era* (1960), quoted a manufacturer's views on the subject: "If a man is dissatisfied, it is his privilege to quit." As the factory system spread, some factories became huge installations, and as multiplant operations began to appear, the instability, informality, arbitrariness, and variability in the relations between labor and management was highlighted. In both the emerging mass-production industries and the older industries with smaller production runs—those characterized by what Philip Scranton called "flexible production"—efforts emerged to impose more order over the chaos of labor relations. From two separate strands there would be woven together in the corporation a new set of much more standardized relationships between management and labor. One of those strands was industrial engineering, often known simply as *Taylorism*; the other was the employee-benefit schemes termed *welfare work*. Eventually these practices would unite under the domain of the personnel department, later renamed the *human resources* department by its professional practitioners.

It was the engineers who first discovered and analyzed the lack of systematic practices in production arrangements. The engineering profession was virtually nonexistent before the great era of canal and railroad construction, and by 1850 there were still only 2,000 civil engineers in the United States. "The rising demand for engineers by industry," wrote Edwin Layton in *The Revolt of the Engineers* (1971), touched off explosive growth in that profession. "The golden age for the application of science to American industry came from 1880 to 1920," Layton noted, "a period which also witnessed the rise of large industrial corporations. In these forty years, the engineering profession increased by almost 2,000 percent, from 7,000 to

136,000 members." From the engineers there came a thorough-going critique of factory management. Beginning in the 1870s, industrial engineers and manufacturers including Henry R. Towne, Henry Metcalfe, and Frederick A. Halsey pioneered what came to be known as the systematic management movement. A variety of engineering journals, such as the *Transactions of the American Society of Mechanical Engineers, Engineering Magazine,* and (later) *System,* published the literature of what Joseph Litterer phrased (in a 1963 article in the *Business History Review*) "the beginnings of a management technology." Managers, these critics pointed out, had almost no control over their production systems under the chaotic regime of the factory system and mass-production technologies of the late nineteenth century. Distanced from an increasingly complex, subdivided, and balkanized production system, managers had yielded too much control to foremen and skilled workers. As a result, the industrial engineers argued, the firms had suffered what Litterer called "organizational uncoupling." The solution was "systematic management," which included massive efforts to learn what the foremen and the craft workers knew of their jobs, to place in management's heads and hands that knowledge of how the jobs were actually done, and if possible to streamline and improve the processes of work.

The work of the industrial engineers who argued for systematic management at first received little attention outside a small circle of professional engineers and managers. Soon, however, this idea moved into the public consciousness through the missionary work of the man who came to symbolize industrial engineering, Frederick W. Taylor. Taylor was a zealous advocate for the new approach to the management of production, and under his leadership systematic management became better known as *scientific management*. From about 1895 until his death in 1915, Taylor publicized his ideas vigorously. Under his leadership the movement took on the overtones of a great crusade. Taylor was the messiah, and his close followers were often referred to as disciples. He offered to troubled business leaders what he called a solution to "the labor problem." Taylor believed that workers responded to only one incentive, money, and that many were naturally prone to do less work than they could. The Taylor system began with the conviction that each worker's particular abilities could be scientifically determined, and every job could be likewise tested to determine a standard day's output from a "first-class worker." The trick, then, was to assign the right employees to the right jobs. The testing of workers and of jobs involved the stopwatches and the time-and-motion studies that soon came to symbolize Taylorism in the public mind. This kind of testing reinforced the seemingly scientific, clinical, objective air of this new, secular religion. So did the complex array of pay schemes. Once those appropriate Taylorite pay incentives were put into place to reward the workers, went the theory, the employees would cheerfully respond with increased productivity. Everyone—employees, bosses, owners, and society in general—would be happier and better off. Here was an elixir for a troubled age.

In a short time Taylorism became famous far and wide as the embodiment of the era's love affair with the idea of efficiency. It seemed to offer a means of restructuring the work environment so as to remove or reduce conflict, improve efficiency, and increase satisfaction by evaluating proficiency on a scientific basis. The stresses and strains of recurrent class conflict could be gotten around by treating everyone objectively and dispassionately. As Samuel Haber pointed out in *Efficiency and Uplift: Scientific Management in the Progressive Era, 1890–1920* (1964), Taylorism allowed the progressives to retain their almost mystical (and elitist) belief in the power of experts while at the same time keeping faith with democratic ideals. Its proponents ranged across the political spectrum and throughout the world. Taylor's admirers even came to include Lenin, who thought that scientific management would fit well with the "scientific socialism" being crafted in the young Soviet Union. Its usefulness seemed to know no bounds, and every sphere from government to forest management and even surgery and baseball were thought to be susceptible to improvement through the application of the Taylorite principles of objective efficiency.

Throughout Europe, as Thomas Hughes noted in *American Genesis: A Century of Invention and Technological Enthusiasm, 1870–1970* (1989), the essence of the genius and the explosive energies of an America emerging as a model for the industrial world in the twentieth century were thought to be bound up in a combination of Taylorism and Fordism. Scientific management and Ford's production system perfected at Highland Park were considered the twin beacons offered by the New World to the Old. As a German phrase of the time stated it, Taylorism plus Fordism equaled Americanism.

Taylorism was in fact not scientific or objective at all, embodying as it did a host of hidden arbitrary assumptions and subjective judgments about jobs and about the people who do them. When Taylor and his disciples were hired by industrialists eager to receive the panacea, what happened in the plants and the offices often was far from what was promised. As Daniel Nelson's *Managers and Workers* has shown, scientific management in any genuine and thorough form was introduced in only a relative handful of plants, and even then not very successfully. It certainly offered no solution to labor-management conflicts, and it was often opposed by middle managers as well as by workers. Nevertheless it had a wide impact in shaping the thinking of generations of engineers and managers on the topic of labor-management relations. It also symbolized the triumph of the idea that efficiency was a decisive value in the dawning age of big business. Its harsh, mechanistic, and materialistic view of human beings in the workplace was soon softened, however, by a process in which it melded with a very different set of practices known as welfare work.

Many middle-class reformers and a fair number of "enlightened" business leaders came to believe that the problems of labor unrest, turnover, and associated social conflicts could best be addressed not through scientific management but through a series of efforts to humanize the corporation and the workplace. This revived an old trend in the history of industrialization, going back to the paternalistic environments of early mill villages and model factory towns such as Lowell, Massachusetts. In the manner of the age, however, the new movement was to be systematic, rational, and efficient.

Employers soon came to experiment with a variety of ways to make life better for the workers both on and off the job by providing an array of educational, recreational, and generally uplifting activities and facilities. These included clean, well-lighted lunchrooms, cafeterias, washrooms, libraries, club houses, YMCAs and YWCAs, sports teams and playing fields, company picnics, factory landscaping, and sometimes extensive company housing or whole idealized towns such as the one the Pullman Palace Car Company built near Chicago. Many firms hired specialists, usually called welfare secretaries, to give direction and impetus to such activities. These specialists were often women with backgrounds in social work and committed to a middle-class vision of an improved and uplifted workforce shaped by the benevolent hand of the caring corporation. Widespread efforts to launch modest pension and profit-sharing plans also marked the era's efforts to build up a feeling of shared interest between the corporation and its employees. Firms such as H. J. Heinz, Pullman, the Filene's department store in Boston, and the National Cash Register Company led the way. The cause was also vigorously promoted by such prominent civic organizations as the League for Social Service and the National Civic Federation. Soon they were joined by universities, which began to offer training courses in welfare practices, and by many in government, as Stuart Brandes noted in his disapproving study, *American Welfare Capitalism, 1880–1940* (1976). In the view of the proponents of welfarism, workers were influenced by far more than the narrow monetary concerns Taylor saw; to improve work and life in an industrial and corporate society, it was necessary to uplift the minds, shape the values, and improve the work, home, and community environments of America's workers and their families.

The movement attracted much attention and support in the business community. Daniel Nelson reported in *Managers and Workers* that "before World War I," at least forty manufacturing firms had "introduced extensive welfare programs" and that "hundreds . . . adopted more modest programs." In a related effort, business and the educational system joined forces to promote vocational training programs in the schools, yet another middle-class effort to shape the working class for more productive and happier lives in the emerging corporate order. The millions of new immigrants from Eastern and Southern Europe, in particular, were the intended beneficiaries of such training and education. In his 1985 study, *Employing Bureaucracy,* Sanford M. Jacoby pointed out that "proponents of industrial education argued that tighter links between the schools and the economy would enable the nation to cope more effectively with the stresses and strains of becoming an industrial urban society." Along with the stronger influences of scientific management and welfare work, the vocational guidance movement would prove to be one of the streams that joined to produce, by about 1920, the new profession of personnel management. Henceforward, according to the most progressive thinking of the day, the chaos and conflict between management and labor would be mitigated. Bureaucracy, order, and efficiency had found a human face: the caring corporation   one big family, supporting a progressive social order in which all could seek improvement and their proper places. Soon there would be, under the aegis of the ubiquitous corporate personnel departments, more uniform systems of hiring, promoting, firing, caring for, and disciplining an increasingly white-collar workforce. Millions of middle-level managers, supervisors, clerks, and operatives would all share relatively similar values and experiences within the world of the corporation, experiencing what Olivier Zunz referred to in *Making America Corporate, 1870–1920* (1990) as "a homogeneous work culture." The old order was giving way to the new, corporate order.

In some sectors, the coming of the corporation also offered new opportunities to women in the workforce, though equality of opportunity and of experience at work remained only a dream. Industrialization and the coming of the corporate order brought a mix of outcomes for women. In the older, agrarian, family-based economy, women had played vital roles in household management and in the production of goods and services such as foodstuffs (e.g., butter and cheese), midwifery, and work as seamstresses and milliners. As industrialization and professionalization took many of these roles away and placed them in the hands of business firms and male professionals, women's economic and social status suffered. The mass production of clothing, for example, reduced women's ownership of proprietorships in the making of hats and dresses. Wendy Gamber's 1997 study, *The Female Economy,* deftly traced those changes in the history of the dressmaking and hatmaking trades from 1860 through 1930. On the other hand, women sometimes found new wage labor opportunities in industry, just as they had done in textiles earlier in the century.

In the corporate era, in response to the pressures of the rapid growth of office staffs, some jobs that had been considered exclusively men's work became the province of women. In the insurance and banking industries, for example, women found employment opportunities in arenas previously closed to them, as Angel Kwolek-Folland's *Engendering Business* (1994) demonstrated. And, as Kwolek-Folland pointed out in her book *Incorporating Women* (1998), "some of the largest gains ever in wage work for young, single women" came after 1880, when there was a "virtual takeover" by women of jobs as "stenographers, typists, and secretaries." There is now a rich literature on women in office jobs, such as Sharon Hartman Strong's *Beyond the Typewriter: Gender, Class, and the Origins of Modern American Office Work, 1900–1930* (1992). Jobs in retailing, including managerial jobs in the new department stores, also often went to women. (Claudia Goldin's *Understanding the Gender Gap* [1990] provided a comprehensive picture of long-term trends of women in the labor force.) Both before and after the rise of big business, most jobs were gendered ones, ones assumed by most people to be either "men's work" or "women's work." Large firms generally used and reinforced prevailing ideas about hierarchies and gender roles to strengthen managerial controls over the workforce. Big businesses hardly saw their principal mission as effecting social justice, but in some industries they did present new opportunities for women and some ethnic groups.

In the realm of the professions, women made some gains, but again these often were confined to lines of work deemed particularly appropriate for women. "By 1900," Angel Kwolek-Folland noted in *Incorporating Women,* "when not quite 1 percent of lawyers and 5 percent of physicians were women, women college graduates began forging entirely new professions." These "women's professions" included social work, teaching, home economics, librarianship, and nursing. All were "less well paid than related professions for men."

In some spheres of both white- and blue-collar work, the corporation's more bureaucratic and systematic approach to hiring sometimes benefited women. As Alice Kessler-Harris noted in *Out to Work: A History of Wage-Earning Women in the United States* (1982), "newly developed techniques such as welfare programs, personnel offices, and scientific management reduced some of the barriers to hiring women." And it was in those dimensions such as personnel offices and welfare work, embodying the "human" sides of the corporation, that big businesses struggled to show a caring, even maternal side. (See Nikki Mandell's 2002 book, *The Corporation as Family.*) Compared to the older, much more self consciously masculine world of physical labor that constituted most skilled work for wages, as well as the all-male precincts of mercantile houses, the corporation sought to present itself as a somewhat more feminine institution. These changes in business, however, made only marginal alterations in the prevailing notions about the proper roles of men and women. In its relationship to gender (as in so many other arenas), the corporation generally used prevailing social norms for its business purposes.

Some cultural historians have seen the rise of the corporate order as producing a devaluation of female authority in American society. In analyzing the complex and multi-layered iconography of American advertising, Jackson Lears found that the symbolic role of women declined as the factory and mass production appeared. Early depictions of the promise and the bounty of agrarian life, what Lears called "the fecund land," gave way to imagery in which women were the passive recipients of the efficient factory, identified as "male-sponsored technological progress." Women similarly lost power, in this view, as the male worlds of science, engineering, and medicine invaded the previously female-controlled arenas of home and the bearing and rearing of children. What had been images of strong mothers or forceful older women in advertising also gave way to portrayals of "giggling teenagers" as advertising shifted its focus toward youth. "By 1910," Lears wrote, "most commonly women in advertisements were merely beneficiaries of the largesse generated by the male genius of mass production." But advertisers quickly devised a new role for women. Production came to be gendered as masculine, consumption as feminine. Eventually, Lears noted, woman "was empowered as an active, desiring subject." And as Helen Damon-Moore's *Magazines for the Millions* (1998) showed, in mass-market publications such as the *Ladies Home Journal* and the *Saturday Evening Post,* editors, advertisers, and many readers embraced the idea that the role of men was to earn a living, while women should be consumers. And it was women's perceived influence as consumers that had helped to open both clerical and managerial jobs for females in such arenas as retail sales, insurance, and banking.

However one see its impact on gender roles and relationships, it seems clear that modern advertising became by the early twentieth century one of the most important pillars in the emerging incorporation of America. It played a key role in the centralization and homogenization of experience that accompanied the rise of big business. Many of the institutions of the new economic order—the mass producers, the mass distributors such as Montgomery Ward and Sears, the early chains such as Woolworth's and the A&P, and the department stores—worked to promote what William Leach in *Land of Desire* (1993) called "a new set of commercial enticements—a commercial aesthetic—to move and sell goods in volume." This was "a commercial aesthetic of desire and longing, . . . a vision of the good life and of paradise." It was not only the images of advertisements that portrayed the new vision of the good life, but a whole array of forms. "After 1880," Leach wrote, "this aesthetic appeared in show windows, electrical signs, fashion shows, advertisements, and billboards; as free services and sumptuous consumer environments; and as the artifacts or commodities themselves." Collectively, all these factors worked together to "suggest a *this*-worldly paradise that was stress-free and 'happy.'" This earthly paradise was to be the environment for a new form of democracy, as more Americans could expect to share in the desire for prosperity and the life it dangled before them.

The new culture built on many traditional American values, such as a fascination with the new and a belief that the privileged United States was as close to paradise as anything on Earth. Consumption and a love for material acquisition had always been part of the culture, but now these aspects became increasingly prominent. Mass production and mass consumption were two sides of the same process; each depended on the other. And it was not just those in big business, advertising, and public relations who saw the growth of mass consumption as an extension of economic and social democracy. An increasing number of Americans shared in the purchase and use of a growing flood of goods and services and the jobs and incomes produced by economic growth. To many shapers of opinion and to many ordinary Americans, there had been a redefinition of what influential progressive writer Herbert Croly called "the promise of American life." That promise, Croly wrote in 1911, consisted primarily of the expectation of "comfort and prosperity for an ever increasing majority of good Americans."

A material paradise on Earth through the work of the beneficent new corporate order became the core of Americans' conception of themselves and their nation, and the core of how those from abroad saw the United States. Raymond Loewy, destined to become the best-known industrial designer of the twentieth century, recalled in his autobiography his reaction on arriving in New York as an immigrant from France in 1919. "I was in a constant state of admiration for the mass of products resulting from superior American technology and drive. I just couldn't believe that there could be such a wealth of productive genius." "The country was flooded," Loewy marveled, "with good, inexpensive things that practically anyone could afford to buy, products which, in Europe, would have been considered sheer luxury." The American Way of Life had emerged.

This vision, it should be emphasized, was widely shared, despite the evidence of worries about big business. Virtually all major social elements in the United States—not just business—embraced it. Soon even the institutions of government, of religion, culture, and education found the idea of a nation devoted to material improvement for the greatest number under corporate leadership an attractive concept. "The new consumer direction of American culture," as William Leach argued, was produced by "alliances among diverse institutions, noneconomic and economic, working together in an interlocking circuit of relationships to reinforce the democratization of desire and the cult of the new." The result was that "the culture of consumer capitalism . . . became over time the very culture of America."

What had at first been deeply troubling to many soon came to seem almost entirely natural to the great majority of Americans. Many within the older segments of the business world (the "proprietary capitalists" among the capitalist class, in Martin Sklar's terms in his 1988 book *The Corporate Reconstruction of American Capitalism, 1890–1916*) soon endorsed and joined the new corporate ways. As Sklar suggested, those who created big business were able to offer much to the old order, building on long-standing American traditions to make the corporation seem the paragon and the beacon of national progress. They thus succeeded in "attaching" to their cause those "from other social sectors—smaller business, politics, the law, the academy, the press, science and engineering, the churches." This process of "class evolution and reintegration helps account," in Sklar's view, for the speed and "relative thoroughness with which centralization directly through the form of corporate consolidation spread in the United States after the depression of the 1890s."

The alliance of business with other powerful social and cultural elements was clearly emergent by the first years of the twentieth century. By that time, for example, many of the big businesses in the high-technology, science-based industries such as the electrical manufacturers, communications companies, machinery producers, and chemical firms had forged strong ties to the institutions of science and technology. Some added to their array of corporate skills and missions the research and development of new products and processes, leading the way to one of the twentieth century's primary engines of economic growth, formal departments of research and development (R&D). The pioneering firms included ones that would remain at the forefront of the application of R&D for decades to come—General Electric, AT&T, Du Pont, Eastman Kodak, and others. David Noble's *America by Design: Science, Technology, and the Rise of Corporate Capitalism* (1977), detailed and analyzed the intimate connections that arose early in the twentieth century among the corporations, the science and engineering establishments, and the nation's universities. The creation of the first true research and development laboratory in the United States, that of General Electric, was emblematic of the web of connections that quickly tied a number of modern corporations to the modern university. At the opening of the twentieth century GE hired to head its R&D operation Willis R. Whitney, a professor of chemistry at MIT (Massachusetts Institute of Technology); by 1906 Whitney's department included more than one hundred employees, many of whom were drawn, like himself, from the university world. All the big businesses that had major stakes in science and engineering came to have strong, ongoing relationships with leading research universities, recruiting staff and consultants in ever-growing numbers as the century progressed. Anyone who has attended or taught at an American university understands the close ties between departments of science and engineering and the corporate community. Their interaction and interdependence played a leading role in shaping research within both the academic and the corporate settings. The needs, values, and priorities of big business came to influence the entire realm of institutions of higher learning. In a similar way, the vocational training movement in particular and the secondary education system in general were designed in part to respond to the corporation's requirements for employees able to meet the daily needs of modern businesses. Education serves many purposes in our society, but none has been thought so vital as that of training young people to take their places as useful members of a productive workforce.

The presence of the corporation was keenly felt even in the heart of the older, agrarian America. The arrival of the railroad in rural communities, mechanization of the farm via the distribution networks of the McCormick Reaper Company and International Harvester, the penetration of agrarian homes by Sears and Montgomery Ward, and the work of agricultural experimental stations all brought the presence of big business and the powerful influence of consumer culture firmly into the heartland. Rural cooperatives did their best to imitate the methods of the new organizations in agribusiness, without yielding (at least at first) to the strong profit orientation of those enterprises. Agrarian civilization in turn had its effects on the corporation in the countryside, as Olivier Zunz points out in his "On the Farm" chapter in *Making America Corporate.* Nevertheless it was the values, technologies, and ways of the corporation that ultimately would prove the strongest influence on the future of rural life. As the twentieth century progressed, farm life as a whole would be revolutionized by the impact of the corporation's tractors, cars and trucks, electric power, and communications systems, as well as its chemical fertilizers, herbicides, and pesticides. The lure of industrial jobs and urban life, along with the declining need for farm labor as a result of mechanization and the widespread consolidation of American farms into fewer but larger concerns, accelerated the long-term decline in the farming population.

It also seemed reasonably clear by the early 1920s that the corporations would prove triumphant over their archenemies, the labor unions. Most of the early big businesses in industry managed to keep unions out through a variety of strategies such as the introduction of new production technologies, the use of political influence and intimidation, high wages, good benefits and other kinds of welfare work, and a willingness to exploit working-class ethnic, racial, and gender divisions. At the end of the nineteenth century the emergence of the American Federation of Labor as the nation's dominant and defining union organization, the "House of Labor," showed that unionism in the United States most often meant craft unions. Under the leadership of Samuel Gompers of the cigarmakers' union before he took leadership of the national union, the affiliated AFL unions soon came to abandon political militancy and to focus on economic gains within the system, a pattern ironically termed *business unionism*. By and large, the membership of the AFL belonged to unions that found life in the older and often declining sectors of the economy such as the construction trades, mining, and the industries still dependent on skilled craft work (such as Gompers's old cigarmakers' union). As David Montgomery argued in *The Fall of the House of Labor*, "by the end of the depression of 1920–2, American workers' militancy had been deflated, trade unionism largely excluded from larger corporate enterprises, and the left wing of the workers' movement isolated from effective mass influence."

Throughout the early twentieth century it was clear how fully almost every powerful element in American life had embraced the new corporate commonwealth. Putting aside their worries about the excesses and abuses that accompanied the rise of big business, influential, well-connected citizens from many walks of life increasingly signaled their willingness to carry the banners of the corporation. A particularly symbolic moment came in 1911, when the Wanamaker's department stores opened their huge new flagship emporium in downtown Philadelphia. Designed by Daniel Burnham—the leading architect of skyscrapers, office buildings, and retail stores in the United States—it stood fifteen stories high and covered an entire city block. It was, Burnham boasted, "the most monumental commercial structure ever erected anywhere in the world. Its total cost exceeded Ten Million Dollars." Leaders from the worlds of business, politics, the professions, religion, and education all gathered to commemorate this grand moment, which marked merchant John Wanamaker's fiftieth anniversary in business.

Presiding over the proceedings was none less than President William Howard Taft. "The President's participation in so high a celebration of American commercial entrepreneurship," noted Thomas S. Hines in *Burnham of Chicago* (1974), "emphasized with pungent clarity the nation's commitment to the capitalist spirit."

And what was the meaning of this new world to ordinary Americans? The corporate-driven, consumer civilization that had emerged by the first part of the twentieth century was sharply highlighted in the brilliant study in cultural anthropology done by Robert S. and Helen Merrell Lynd and published as *Middletown: A Study in American Culture* (1929). The Lynds and their field staff conducted intensive investigations in 1924–25 in Muncie, Indiana, the community they would call Middletown in their book. Their goal was to compare life as it had been lived in the 1880s to the way it was lived in the mid-1920s, and their work has held up well. They focused on activities such as getting a living, making a home, training the young, leisure, religious practices, and community activities. Their portrait of Middletown illustrated the vast transformation that had swept over the nation since big business arose in industry and helped effect the range of changes discussed above.

The Lynds' major finding was that the meaning of life in Middletown in 1924 was dominated by "getting a living." "The money medium of exchange and the cluster of activities associated with its acquisition drastically condition the other activities of the people," they concluded. Society had come to be divided into two groups, which the Lynds designated the "working class and business class." The two groups kept different hours, went to different churches ("Holy Roller or Presbyterian"), belonged to different clubs, and drove different cars (Fords or Buicks). But despite these differences, both groups gave their primary allegiance to the getting of "the money medium of exchange." The Lynds found those in the business class somewhat more satisfied than the working class with their jobs and the higher prestige they enjoyed in the community, but "for very many" in both groups "the amount of robust satisfaction they derive from the actual performance of their specific jobs seems, at best, to be slight." Labor Day had declined from its high place in the 1890s, unions played a much less important role as providers of social functions, and "public opinion" was "no longer with organized labor."

Since psychological satisfaction was now found less often on the job, Americans increasingly focused on leisure, home, and community activities in the search for meaning in their lives. Material progress was in fact providing much more in the way of leisure time and the other good things that could be bought, from household appliances to cars to countless other goods and services. "For both working and business class no other accompaniment of getting a living approaches in importance the money received for their work." The consumer society had come to offer what meaning life afforded for most. "The rise of large-scale advertising, popular magazines, movies, radio, and other channels of increased cultural diffusion from without" the Lynds wrote, "are rapidly changing habits of thought as to what things are essential to living and multiplying optional occasions for spending money." This was the answer to the question posed in *Middletown*'s seventh chapter, "Why do they work so hard?"

For numerous critics of modern life, this was a deplorable, even a calamitous, outcome. Many blamed big business for engendering such a materialistic, unrewarding, and alienating society. David Noble's 1977 work, *America by Design,* for example, was a thoughtful and forcefully argued critique of corporate civilization and its alliance with the institutions of technology and science. "Modern Americans," in Noble's view, "confront a world in which everything changes, yet nothing moves. The perpetual rush to novelty that characterizes the modern marketplace, with its escalating promise of technological transcendence, is matched by the persistence of pre-formed patterns of life which promise merely more of the same." The result, he argued, is "a remarkably dynamic society that goes nowhere." Though they were careful to strike a tone of scientific objectivity in *Middletown*, the Lynds clearly shared many of those same concerns. So have many thoughtful critics of modern life.

Whether there were (and are) meaningful and realistic alternatives to a materialist-based civilization in the United States is a difficult question. From at least the time of the Great Awakening in the middle of the eighteenth century, reformers have preached to the American people about the emptiness of materialism and have sought to lift their vision to some higher plane. On the whole these efforts have fallen on deaf ears.

Certainly the corporation was not the original cause of Americans' devotion to materialism. That value had always been present, but by the early twentieth century it seemed to crowd out others even more insistently. Big business arose, as we have seen, not merely because evil and clever robber barons pulled the wool over our eyes. Nor did it flourish without arousing doubt, criticism, and opposition. The political worries about the dangers posed by big business led to a new level of economic activism by government, though that brought a somewhat muddled and often contradictory set of results. The modern corporation very quickly became the dominant institutional form in American life, forming deep and complex ties with other institutions. The corporation's ways, methods, technological systems, and core values soon affected almost every aspect of daily life in the twentieth-century United States. Despite the doubts and pain it provoked, its victory came relatively quickly. Perhaps that is what President Calvin Coolidge meant by his famous and cryptic remark that the business of America is business.

Big business arose and triumphed in so many critical industries because it was the most effective instrument to organize and coordinate large-scale, productive economic activities in a nation where material progress was emerging as the principal purpose of life. Once the transportation and communications networks of the nineteenth century were put in place, when the highly productive technologies of the Second Industrial Revolution appeared, it became possible and profitable to build industrial businesses that occupied many sites, carried out many functions, and served many markets. The potential of new technologies and of scientific research could then be fully unleashed, and for the first time it became possible to produce more than the economy could absorb. Ironically, at the time when humankind could at last see the way to provide material goods in abundance, society faced another sort of difficulty altogether. The potential for instability and chaos through overproduction, price wars, and harrowing cycles of boom-and-bust was soon clear to manufacturers and to many others as well. Efforts to overcome those problems while retaining the productive potential of science and technology were a central part of the overall economic and social quest in America, what Robert Wiebe termed the search for order. Despite the genuine and fierce political debates of the era, an outcome of compromise was understandable. Given their political traditions, it was unlikely that Americans would accept either of the two extremes of destroying big business through antitrust or adopting state ownership or thoroughgoing oversight of the economy.

Largely through the two paths we traced earlier, vertical and horizontal integration, a prolific generation of business leaders in the United States created a new organizational form, one that had not existed at the close of the Civil War outside a handful of major railroads. A few examples appeared in industry in the 1880s and early 1890s. Legal changes encouraged centralized firms, and important shifts in the financial system facilitated mergers. The depression of the 1890s put renewed pressure on prices and greatly speeded the formation of large firms, particularly in the newer industries that employed mass production, capital-intensive technologies and struggled with the resulting excess capacity. By the end of the Great Merger Wave in 1905, big business was in place in the center economy. Within another decade or so, it was clear how deeply big business had affected government, labor-management relations, science and technology, the institutions of higher learning, patterns of gender and race, as well as the daily lives of millions of ordinary Americans, as the *Middletown* study dramatically underscored.

Those who deplored society's acceptance of big business—its values and its practices—reflected genuine and deeply felt doubts and fears. The subsequent history of American economic growth and the continuing triumph of materialism, however, has shown what the vast majority of Americans seem to want—certainly not all they want, but what they want most. Nor is this a peculiarity of the United States. Big business arose in a roughly similar form in Western Europe, with some differences in timing and particulars. On the whole, however, the similarities in the forms, functions, and activities of big businesses around the world seem greater than the differences. Because the integrated corporation proved to be the most effective means yet created for addressing the remarkably widespread conviction that material progress was the principal *raison d'être* of modern industrial societies, it emerged as a central feature of contemporary civilization. Despite deep doubts of the sort voiced by Americans earlier, and despite recurrent ominous signs that uncontrolled economic expansion imperils the planet's ecosystems, the lure of industrial capitalism seems ever stronger.

And so it appeared to historian Henry Adams in *The Education of Henry Adams* as he reflected on the triumph of industrial civilization when he visited the great World's Fairs at Chicago (1893), Paris (1900), and St. Louis (1904). Such grand international expositions were popular showcases for the world's cultures and products throughout the last half of the nineteenth century, and Adams was among the many millions who saw and marveled at them. The fairs were also stages for the emerging great corporations, such as the Pennsylvania Railroad, General Electric, Siemens, Westinghouse, and Krupp, which placed exhibitions at many of the expositions that followed the pioneering great World's Fair, London's Crystal Palace Exhibition of 1851. At the Paris Exposition of 1900 Adams observed "the complexities of the new Daimler motor, and of the automobile, which, since 1893, had become a nightmare at a hundred kilometres an hour." What moved him most, however, was "the great hall of dynamos," the generators of the wondrous new energy form of the age, electricity. For Adams the dynamo "became a symbol of infinity, . . . a moral force." "The planet itself," wrote Adams, "seemed less impressive, in its old-fashioned, deliberate, annual or daily revolution, than this huge wheel, revolving within an arm's length at some vertiginous speed, and barely murmuring—scarcely humming an audible warning to stand a hair's breadth further for respect of power—while it would not wake the baby lying close against its frame. Before the end, one began to pray to it." Here the capitalistic, centralizing, and mechanical civilization of the West raised a monument to its new gods—science and technology, organization, and the corporation.

For Henry Adams, the history of Western civilization was divisible into only two eras, which he symbolized through the imagery of the Virgin (or Venus) and the Dynamo. From the beginnings of Western civilization, the dominant force was the Virgin—the mystery of fecundity and religion, or what Adams called "love of God and lust for power in a future life." With the coming of the scientific revolution and the rise of technology that began in the Renaissance, however, humankind in the West began to embrace a new, secular faith. Materialism, the machine, and finally the corporation brought the triumph of that new faith in the forces he saw embodied in the Dynamo. And "the Trusts and the Corporations," he gloomily concluded in his autobiography, "stood for the larger part of the new power that had been created since 1840. . . . They were revolutionary, troubling all the old conventions and values, as the screws of ocean steamers must trouble a school of herring." The large corporation had emerged as the most powerful institution of a civilization that worshipped the force of the Dynamo. It still is.

As we struggle with the problems and the dangers that accompany the corporate cornucopia, we will likely do so with the methods, institutions, and habits of mind that have shaped our industrial, corporate civilization. We have cast our lot with the corporation, the engineer, and the scientist. Together we have made a material, technical world, as Adams sensed while standing before the dynamo in Paris, on the cusp between the nineteenth and the twentieth centuries. To break out of this world would require that we adopt fundamentally new values, as Adams believed the Western world had done by gradually but decisively shifting its allegiance from the Virgin to the Dynamo. Such changes are possible, but they do not happen easily, and they do not happen often.

BIBLIOGRAPHICAL ESSAY

Although historians and many others in America have long agreed that business has played a central role in the history of the United States, its place in the study of American history has never been central. Throughout most of the period during which professional historians have sought to understand and explain their nation's history, they focused on the political events and personalities of the past. The colonizing of the eastern coast by Europeans, the struggle for political and cultural independence from Great Britain, the rise and evolution of political parties, the expansion of the physical boundaries of the United States and the settlement of those new areas by European immigrants, the conflicts between the various regions or sections of the nation, and the country's diplomatic affairs and its wars—these events seemingly constituted American history. The focus was primarily political, and on the whole the actors in the story were eminent, white, and male (Great White Men, as later critics put it). In part because of the powerful impact of the work of historian Frederick Jackson Turner emphasizing the influence of the frontier in shaping America, many came to feel that the history of the United States was distinctive, indeed almost unique, as compared to that of the European nations. The common experience of conquering a continent and building a civilization from the wilderness, many historians argued, helped to make the United States more egalitarian, democratic, and open than the European societies from which it sprang. Business was seen as having played only an incidental role in the story.

Because most historians traditionally conceptualized the American past as a struggle for ever-more democratic political forms and the extension of economic opportunity to increasingly more citizens, they tended to view business as a negative, excessively conservative force. Except for occasional episodes such as the struggle over the nature of the banking system in the early decades of the nineteenth century, historians seldom viewed business as central to the American story. With the rise of big business that changed. Once large-scale enterprises appeared in the American economy, they began to attract both political attention and increasing notice, and criticism, from historians. Our perspective on the rise of big business has undergone a number of shifts since Americans first began to think and write about these giant institutions. From the initial appearance of large-scale firms until the 1970s, most of both the public and the scholarly discourse about their societal role centered on the best way to discipline and control such powerful private interests in a democratic society. Americans worried and argued about robber barons and trust building even as big business continued to develop into the most dominant, influential institution in our society.

In the era following World War II, the modern corporation, along with the United States military, became the most important vehicle through which American influence was projected around the globe. Among professional historians, the prevailing analytical framework came to be the "consensus" school. Powerfully influenced by the experience of World War II and the climate of the Cold War, historians emphasized another variant of the idea of American uniqueness. Building on the insights of Alexis de Tocqueville's *Democracy in America,* scholars such as Louis Hartz, Richard Hofstadter, and Daniel Boorstin argued that the United States had on the whole been "born free" of the European conflicts over class and property. Because Americans never had to undergo the crisis of a struggle to displace an established aristocracy based on birth and never had any truly serious disagreements over the desirability of private property and competition, the United States was thought to have enjoyed a remarkably wide consensus over fundamental political and economic issues. The basic purpose of the society was to be the pursuit of material growth, its fundamental decision-making process was to be democratic, and there was to be a relatively high degree of freedom of individual political expression. Within that wide and deep consensus there had of course been many struggles. But those conflicts had been waged over questions less basic than the ones that divided European countries that had fought bloody revolutions to uproot privileged aristocracies and then had remained locked until near the end of the twentieth century in a grim struggle over whether capitalism or communism would ultimately define their societies.

Despite the broad agreement on the desirability of private property and capitalism, however, business continued to be seen by American historians as a negative, threatening force, with the business community acting primarily as a brake slowing the long-term progress toward a more nearly equal and free society. Business was regarded as perhaps the closest thing in the American past to the evil tradition of aristocratic privilege in Europe. Big business was seen as a persistent threat because of its great power and influence in American society. The corporation was a dangerous beast that had to be tamed or caged by the countervailing political power of liberal, left-oriented political movements such as those of the progressives and Franklin D. Roosevelt's New Deal in the 1930s. The apparatus of regulation and the antitrust laws (put in place beginning in the 1880s) and the welfare state of the 1930s represented political efforts to discipline large-scale business enterprise and soften the sharper edges of an individualistic, harshly competitive economic system.

In the 1960s Americans experienced another powerful wave of concern about the abuse of private economic power. This produced the scholarship of the New Left, manifested in such works as Gabriel Kolko's harsh indictment of the liberal tradition and its view of progressivism, *The Triumph of Conservatism* (1963). Criticism from the left crested at a time when the American corporation was reaching its zenith in the markets of the world. Indeed, so strong did U.S. business seem to the rest of the world that one of the most popular issues abroad was how to respond to what many saw as the dangerous growth of American economic and cultural imperialism. One of the most popular and influential books of the era, Jean-Jacques Servan-Schreiber's *The American Challenge* (1968), voiced Europeans' deep anxieties about the spread of American business overseas. At home, Americans both loved and feared the corporation, but few at that time regarded it as weak or incompetent.

As the relative power of the United States waned during the 1970s and 1980s, Americans came to regard big business in a rather different light. Not only had it become an accepted part of the cultural landscape, it now seemed less threatening. By the early 1990s, many observers saw the corporations of other societies, especially Japan, as superior in a number of respects to American ones. Thereafter, however, American business demonstrated once more its resilience and strength. Many of the large, integrated firms that had arisen in the early world of giant enterprises, as well as new ones, responded to changed competitive conditions and became less integrated and relatively smaller and leaner. By the early twenty-first century, American business seemed once more on top of the world. Thomas K. McCraw, *American Business, 1920–2000: How It Worked* (2000) analyzed the triumphs of American business through its international ups, downs, and ups in the twentieth century.

As in so many other aspects of national life, Americans have become more aware of the international context in which the modern corporation arose in the United States. Although America led the way in the creation of big business and its dominance of contemporary industrial and postindustrial society, other nations clearly experienced many of the same developments, though in somewhat different patterns and often at later points in time. One of the effects of the heightened perception of these similarities was to erode further the belief in America's uniqueness, which contributed to the decline of the consensus school of American historiography. In addition, the social conflicts of the 1960s and the increasing tendency of historians to analyze history with regard to particular sectors of society (especially women, racial and ethnic minorities, and ordinary Americans) rather than to attempt to interpret the history of the society as a whole made it increasingly difficult to understand the American past from any overarching point of view.

Against the backdrop of these trends in the writing of American history in general, the analysis of the rise of big business after the 1950s came with few exceptions to be the province of specialists in business and economic history. And much more than that of any other scholar, the work of Alfred D. Chandler, Jr., dominated our understanding of this topic.

Chandler's most influential early work was a seminal article in the *Business History Review* (1959) on the beginnings of big business, and his 1962 book, *Strategy and Structure*. These pathbreaking contributions signaled the decline in scholarly interest in the "robber barons or industrial statesmen" approach to the topic. The first historical "school" dealing with the rise of big business (and one that still dominates popular versions of the history of this topic) was formed by the writers emphasizing the immoral and socially irresponsible role of the "robber barons." Charles Francis Adams, Jr., and his brother Henry set the tone for much later writing in their assessment of the shady hijinks of early American railroad moguls, *Chapters of Erie* (1886). The brothers Adams blended revulsion with perhaps a pinch of secret admiration, and their lively treatment is still highly readable today. Henry Demarest Lloyd's *Wealth Against Commonwealth* (1894) was an early assault on one of the nation's most closely studied corporations, Standard Oil (now Exxon). Lloyd's perspective was that of what might be termed "Christian socialism," and many other historians of this school have shared a similar inclination. A bible for such interpretations was Gustavus Myers's three-volume *History of the Great American Fortunes* (1907–1910), which attacked the methods by which prominent business leaders had acquired their great wealth. After a decline during World War I and the inhospitable 1920s, this critical interpretation was revived during the Great Depression. Matthew Josephson published what became the standard work of this school, *The Robber Barons: The Great American Capitalists, 1861–1901* (1934). In Josephson's view, a handful of business pirates unscrupulously fought their way to controlling much of the nation's economy, and (as he argued four years later in *The Politicos*) of the nation's political apparatus as well. This way of looking at the history of business proved remarkably resilient, particularly in the general textbooks of American history and in American history survey classes. It even had influence in the way those in other nations regard the United States, as demonstrated by such studies as Marianne Debouzy's *Le Capitalisme "Sauvage" aux Etats-Unis, 1860–1900* (1972).

During the 1940s and 1950s, the opposing view was represented by the school known as the "industrial statesman" historians. Writing at the time of America's and American business's dominance of the postwar world, these scholars emphasized the heroic achievements of the generation of business leaders who built big businesses. They pointed to the efficiency of rationalized competition and its role in expanded economic growth. Then, too, the Cold War had its effect. The postwar era was one in which many people thought of economic growth as a weapon in the global conflict with communism (the clearest sign of that was the wide influence of cold warrior Walt Rostow's *The Stages of Economic Growth: A Non-Communist Manifesto,* 1960). Historians who emphasized the positive achievements of big businesses almost always saw those accomplishments in significant measure as personal triumphs, the work of extraordinary individuals. Most of the "industrial statesmen" group, in fact, were biographers. Such laudatory works as Allan Nevins's *John D. Rockefeller: The Heroic Age of American Enterprise*

(1941), Ralph and Muriel Hidy's *Pioneering in Big Business, 1882–1911* (1955), also about Rockefeller and his associates, and Julius Grodinsky's *Jay Gould* (1957) reinforced the idea that big business was the work of a generation of men of uncommon ability. Relatively little attention was given to trying to understand and explain patterns in the evolution of large corporations. Politics and personalities continued to comprise the lens through which the rise of big business was usually viewed. The generation of giants who founded early big businesses have continued to attract the attention of talented biographers ever since, as illustrated by such examples as Ron Chernow's fine life of Rockefeller (*Titan*, 1998), Jean Strouse's *Morgan* (1999), and Douglas Brinkley's focus on Henry Ford in *Wheels for the World* (2003).

Other approaches to the history of American business did emerge, but they captured the imagination neither of general historians nor of the broad public as did the good-versus-evil pairing of "robber barons or industrial statesmen." For example, Thomas C. Cochran tried over a long and distinguished career to direct historians' attention to the social context and consequences of business's influence in American life. Cochran produced an extensive, excellent body of studies from the 1940s into the 1970s that analyzed the interaction between business and other institutions in society, including religion and education. Perhaps the book that best summarized Cochran's ideas and his sociological approach to history was his *Business in American Life: A History* (1972). Although many American historians would follow Cochran's lead into social history from the 1960s on, his work led to the founding of no "school" of business history.

Business historians also found little of interest in the approach of the "New Economic History" that utilized economic theory and statistical analysis. That new approach certainly swept the field of economic history in the United States, as is apparent in the contents of the Economic History Association's *Journal of Economic History* from the early 1960s on. Methodological disagreements and unfamiliar sets of questions kept business historians from seeing very much of real use in the New Economic History. In the United States, the study of business history has largely remained more the work of persons trained in university departments of history rather than in departments of economics, and many historians resisted the theoretical and econometric approach. Louis Galambos's quantitative content analysis study, *The Public Image of Big Business, 1880–1940* (1975) was an exception, and so was the work of his student, Naomi Lamoreaux, as in her study, *The Great Merger Movement in American Business, 1895–1904* (1985). Overall, however, historians of business have made only limited use of economic theory in attacking questions about business enterprise in the American past.

The work that did shape the field of business history in a fundamental way was, of course, that of Alfred Chandler. His Pulitzer Prize–winning 1977 study, *The Visible Hand: The Managerial Revolution in American Business,* provided the most complete statement of his ideas about the rise of big business in the United States. That work proved highly influential, not only for the study of business history in the United States but throughout the world. No other historian has ever exercised such a strong influence over the study of business history as did Chandler. Virtually every work now written on the history of modern, large-scale enterprise must begin by positioning itself in relation to the Chandlerian analytical framework. Over the course of more than four decades, Chandler's prodigious and highly focused scholarship yielded a body of work that virtually became business history. He directed his great energies at essentially a single set of interrelated questions. Like Ahab pursuing the White Whale, Chandler tenaciously pursued the large corporation. He sought to answer these questions: When, where, and why did it arise? How did it persist? Where did it spread? How was it organized? What functions did it perform? So influential was this approach that it almost crowded out other questions and methodologies. It reinforced the already strong tendency for historians to think of the history of business from the late-nineteenth century on as the history of big business and of mass production and to begin by asking how many individual firms or industries had histories that fit into the structuralist-functionalist or strategic-structural framework. (For a summary of Chandler's ideas, see Thomas K. McCraw, ed., *The Essential Alfred Chandler: Essays toward a Historical Theory of Big Business,* 1988.)

Chandler's approach proved influential among a wide circle of historians and others in disciplines such as business administration. (It was my privilege to be Chandler's student, and his work strongly influenced this book). Indeed, there grew up over time a related set of historical studies that collectively represent what Louis Galambos has termed the *organizational synthesis.* Galambos summed up his ideas on this body of historiography in two influential essays in the *Business History Review,* "The Emerging Organizational Synthesis in Modern American History" (1970), and an update, "Technology, Political Economy, and Professionalization: Central Themes of the Organizational Synthesis" (1983). This interpretive framework, Galambos wrote in the second of those essays, emphasized "organization building, both public and private, and the creation of new and elaborate networks of formal, hierarchical structures of authority that gradually came to dominate our economy, polity, and culture."

This trend in time carried historians' interests outside the "internalist" focus of Alfred Chandler's work. In particular, topics in labor history, the history of work, of the role of government and women's roles in the economy, and above all, the history of technology have expanded our view of the meaning of big business's growth. The interdisciplinary work of Philip Scranton (*Proprietary Capitalism,* 1983, *Figured Tapestry,* 1989, and *Endless Novelty,* 1997) reminded us that much of American history in the last century involved industries that did not fit the dominant paradigm of big business and mass production. Still, those topics remain at the heart of the "organizational synthesis."

In the years since the appearance of Chandler's *Visible Hand,* there have been many criticisms of his work. After his move in the early 1970s to the presentist and triumphalist environment of the Harvard Business School (the "West Point of

Capitalism"), Chandler pressed his original insights beyond the period and culture from which he had initially drawn them. In *Scale and Scope: The Dynamics of Industrial Capitalism* (1990) and in other work after *The Visible Hand,* he argued that the American patterns he had analyzed up to the Great Depression extended through subsequent decades, applied to a wide range of other national experiences as well, and were linked to broad patterns of economic growth. Most of the criticism of his scholarship in recent decades has focused on this later portion of his work. For example, William Parker's 1991 review of *Scale and Scope* in the *Journal of Economic History* acknowledged that "Between 1880 and 1929—possibly even to 1950—the managerial decisions important for a growing output and efficiency were related to the management of techniques, equipment, markets, and management itself." After 1940, however, Parker and others found the argument significantly less persuasive. Still others objected to what they saw as the implied inevitability of the outcomes Chandler traced and to the idea that the large, integrated, diversified firm ("the modern corporation") was the final, perfect form of corporate evolution. (See Richard R. John's review essay, "Elaborations, Revisions, Dissents: Alfred D. Chandler, Jr.'s *The Visible Hand* after Twenty Years," in the 1997 *Business History Review*; Naomi R. Lamoreaux, Daniel M. G. Raff, and Peter Temin, "Beyond Markets and Hierarchies: Toward a New Synthesis of American Business History," in the 2000 *American Historical Review,* and the essays on Chandler in *Enterprise and Society* in 2004. Some economic analysts, such as Naomi Lamoreaux (see her essay in the second volume of the *Cambridge Economic History of the United States*) emphasized the market power of firms in oligopolistic industries and the inflexibility of large enterprises as technical innovators. Nevertheless, most of Chandler's critics among economists accept his basic explanatory framework for the *initial* rise of big business, even if they doubt his arguments about the mid-to-late-twentieth-century economy. Some of those scholars have sought to place the economic contributions of the large firm within a theoretical framework emphasizing the importance of information and the reduction of transactions costs within the firm. The work of Oliver Williamson, Ronald Coase, and Douglass North has been particularly central in that regard, and Chandler incorporated some of those ideas in his own work. Indeed, there is much shared ground between Chandler and many of his critics in the economics profession.

A number of scholars working primarily in economics have contributed studies exploring the circumstances in which cartel-like arrangements did or (more often) did not prove very effective competitive tools. Among these, Margaret Levenstein's "Mass Production Conquers the Pool: Firm Organization and the Nature of Competition in the Nineteenth Century," in the *Journal of Economic History* (1995) was particularly fine. Her treatment of the rise of Dow Chemical was especially suggestive concerning the relationships between barriers to entry and the coming of the mass-producers. (See also her 1998 book, *Accounting for Growth: Information Systems and the Creation of the Large Corporation.*) The creation of barriers to entry through effective marketing was also well illustrated in Nancy F. Koehn's essay, "Henry Heinz and Brand Creation in the Late Nineteenth Century," in the 1999 *Business History Review.*

An important group of critics of the Chandlerian framework came largely from sociology rather than economics. These analysts, such as Gerald Berk, Michael J. Piore, Charles F. Sabel, Neil Fligstein, and Jonathan Zeitlin, have disagreed with the Chandlerian framework on much more fundamental grounds than have most economists. These more profound critics have argued that there were plausible and workable alternatives to mass production and economic concentration, and that political and economic muscle had more to do with the triumph of the corporation than efficiency. A similar dissent using "power theory" in political sociology was William G. Roy's *Socializing Capital: The Rise of the Large Industrial Corporation in America* (1997), which posited that the "advantages of size were at least as much a matter of the power" wielded by the capitalist class "as any efficiencies they may have enjoyed." Charles Perrow's *Organizing America: Wealth, Power, and the*

Origins of Corporate Capitalism (2002) is another such critique. Many of those who find Chandler's work fundamentally unpersuasive believe that there were numerous other potential paths and contingencies that could have produced very different outcomes than the one Chandler traced.

Much of the argument marshaled by those scholars turned on the manifold changes in the legal system that furthered the spread of large corporations. Partly because of federalism and the resulting snarl of both state and federal laws, the long-run impact of the law on business is a topic of such complexity that it almost seems to defy generalization. Tony A. Freyer's essay "Business Law and American Economic History," in the second volume of the *Cambridge Economic History of the United States* (2000) makes that clear. It does seem apparent that since the days of Chief Justice John Marshall, American law "within broad limits always has been instrumental to American economic development," as Freyer put it. The many ways in which the law accommodated and encouraged the corporate order from the Civil War to the Progressive Era, in the views of such intellectual heirs of Matthew Josephson as William Roy, Charles Perrow, et al., simply represented the wealth and power of capitalist interests calling the tune. While there are clearly some persuasive elements in that interpretation, it fails to recognize the law's persistent responsiveness to broad changes in American attitudes about what sort of institutional and legal environment seemed most likely to foster economic development. As the nation grew more urban and industrial, and as economic and technical changes made larger-scale economic units seem more promising avenues to growth, jobs, and rising incomes than family farms and small businesses, the law shifted its stance to foster "the growth of managerial capitalism," according to Freyer. This "benefited middle-class groups in the form of lower consumer prices and new entrepreneurial opportunities under more regularized contract and property law." These changes were gradual and often existed alongside judicial rulings that contradicted this trend, which made the legal landscape so complex and convoluted. Freyer has emphasized that many of the most critical legal changes in question came before, not during or after, the great merger wave and so are difficult to attribute to the power of the new order. The overriding question in the long run was: which legal rules best fitted the evolving promise of American life? Rather than simply reflecting the power of corporate interests, the business-related legal changes from the Civil War to World War I are perhaps best understood as a further evolution of what J. Willard Hurst characterized as the law's efforts to release entrepreneurial energy in nineteenth-century America. While scholars such as Perrow, Roy, and Fligstein do not see the rise of big business as representing economic promise for the nation, many in the American legislatures and courts of the late nineteenth and early twentieth centuries did, and not just because the corporate interests had power.

Since big business arose primarily as a means of creating, expanding, and controlling an increasingly technical economy and society, it was natural that scholars paid a great deal of attention to the history of modern technology. The work of Lewis Mumford, especially his *Technics and Civilization* (1934), gave structure to the topic and did much to launch the discipline of the history of technology. Siegfried Giedion's *Mechanization Takes Command* (1948) gave a broad and rich account of the coming of the machine age and was a pioneering study in the history of everyday life. More recently the major work was that of Thomas P. Hughes, who has highlighted and analyzed the role of invention, the rise of complex technical systems, technological momentum, and the broad cultural impact of modern technology. Beginning with his biography of *Elmer Sperry: Inventor and Engineer* (1971), Hughes crafted a remarkable body of scholarship. His *Networks of Power: Electrification in Western Society, 1880–1930* (1983) broke new ground in the transnational, comparative study of scientific and technical systems that are interwoven with both economics and politics. Although he explicitly denies that complex technical systems are autonomous, Hughes's work nevertheless argues that "it is difficult to change the direction of large electric power systems— and perhaps that of large sociotechnical systems in general."

Like that of Chandler, Hughes's work causes the reader to consider the possibility that technological determinism shapes history, though both men take pains to disassociate themselves from that suggestion. With *American Genesis* (1989) Hughes offered a new synthesis emphasizing the central role of inventors, industrial scientists, engineers, and designers in the making of America after 1870. His *Human-Built World: How to Think about Technology and Culture* (2004), synthesized major patterns in the history of American technology and culture, through the information age.

The vital importance of science-based, high-technology industries in modern economies has drawn the attention of many other historians of technology. Hugh G. J. Aitken's two books on radio (*Syntony and Spark—The Origins of Radio,* 1976 and *The Continuous Wave,* 1985) traced the subtle interactions among science, technology, and the marketplace. The history of research and development in the modern corporation was analyzed in many studies, including Reese V. Jenkins, *Images and Enterprise: Technology and the American Photographic Industry* (1975), George Wise, *Willis R. Whitney, General Electric, and the Origins of U.S. Industrial Research* (1985), Leonard S. Reich, *The Making of American Industrial Research: Science and Business at GE and Bell, 1876–1926* (1985), and David A. Hounshell and John Kenly Smith, Jr., *Science and Corporate Strategy: Du Pont R&D, 1902–1980* (1988). All gave clear evidence of the intimate connections between the modern corporations in science-based industries and the institutions of science and technology, especially the universities. David Noble's *Amer-ica by Design: Science, Technology, and the Rise of Corporate Capitalism* (1977) presented a sharply critical account of the nexus among business, engineers, and scientists in the twentieth century. Other important contributions from historians of technology included David A. Hounshell, *From the American System to Mass Production, 1800–1932: The Development of Manufacturing Technology in the United States* (1984), which analyzed a major strain in the history of mass production, from the federal armories of the early republic through the automobile industry. Much remains to be explored on the historical ground where the military, business, and technology met, but one can find important contributions in the chapter entitled "Brain Mill for the Military" in Thomas Hughes's *American Genesis: A Century of Invention and Technological Enthusiasm, 1870–1970* and the essays in Merritt Roe Smith, ed., *Military Enterprise and Technological Change: Perspectives on the American Experience* (1985). Steven W. Usselman's *Regulating Railroad Innovation* (2002) was a superb blending of the history of technology and of business, and it broke new ground in analyzing the technical conservatism and long-run economic vulnerability of large enterprises committed to a prevailing technological system. The essay by Stanley L. Engerman and Kenneth L. Sokoloff, "Technology and Industrialization, 1790–1914," in the *Cambridge Economic History of the United States* (2000), provided an excellent summary of how economists have conceptualized and measured the central role of technical change in nineteenth-century American economic history. Engerman and Sokoloff also discussed the changing structure of the business firm and competition over the course of that century.

The literature on other topics tied to the rise of big business, such as Taylorism, work, the changing nature of the workforce, and labor-management relations, is vast. The body of work dealing with unions and strikes is even more vast, though the role of unions in industries dominated by big business was not great before the New Deal. There is room here to mention only a few sources. Joseph Litterer's 1963 article in the *Business History Review,* "Systematic Management: Design for Organizational Recoupling in American Manufacturing Firms," is the beginning point in any study of systematic management. Frederick W. Taylor and his followers have been the subjects of many articles and books. Hugh G. J. Aitken's *Taylorism at Watertown Arsenal* (1960) was an early case study that remains highly useful. An invaluable account of the rise of the engineering profession, the engineer's relation to business, and the ideology of engineering was contributed by Edwin T. Layton, Jr, in his oddly titled book, *The Revolt of the Engineers: Social Re-*

sponsibility and the American Engineering Profession (1971). Layton focused on the conflicts between the demands of business and the engineering profession's ethical demands; most readers will conclude that the engineers did not revolt but instead soft-pedaled their commitment to social responsibility. Daniel Nelson's *Managers and Workers: Origins of the New Factory System in the United States, 1880–1920* (1975) was a balanced and thorough treatment of the technological, managerial, and personnel changes that affected the workplace in the period covered in this book. Robert Kanigel's 1997 biography of Taylor, *The One Best Way,* explored the concept of efficiency, so important to the rise of big business. David Montgomery's *The Fall of the House of Labor: The Workplace, the State, and American Labor Activism, 1865–1925* (1987) provided a rich, wide-ranging look at the struggles over control of the shop floor, the new management systems and styles, the political milieu, and the battles between unions and management that left the AFL in a rigid and weakened condition by the beginning of the 1920s. Montgomery's study looks backward into the nineteenth century, while Sanford M. Jacoby's *Employing Bureaucracy: Managers, Unions, and the Transformation of Work in American Industry, 1900–1945* (1985) looks forward from turn-of-the-century events toward the mid-twentieth-century state of labor and management. Jacoby's work is particularly strong on the topic of the creation of modern personnel practices and the workings of labor "markets" inside the corporation.

Life inside the corporation is the focus of a growing body of literature that continues to move beyond an interest in the political context and the conflicts between unions and management. JoAnne Yates's *Control through Communication: The Rise of System in American Management* (1989) was a good example of this, demonstrating in tangible detail the ways in which modern organizations were able to record, transmit, summarize, and communicate data and decisions throughout highly complex bureaucracies. Alongside works such as that of Sanford Jacoby, mentioned above, Yates's in-depth look at the inner workings of bureaucracy gives us an even better understanding of the day-to-day functions of big business.

The task of fitting big business into the surrounding social and cultural context is one that still calls for vastly more attention. Again, the work of Lewis Mumford and Siegfried Giedion are essential beginning points. Thomas Hughes's contributions on the cultural impact of mechanization, design, and architecture in industry were a further reminder of the riches that can be mined by historians exploring the interconnections between big business, technology, and the social matrix from which they sprang. Martin J. Sklar's *The Corporate Reconstruction of American Capitalism, 1890–1916: The Market, the Law, and Politics* (1988) offered a careful, learned, and complex argument that explored changes in class relations, ideas about the market, and shifts in the laws governing property. Sklar explained the nuances in several variants of what he and others called corporate liberalism, as embodied in the views of Theodore Roosevelt, William Howard Taft, and Woodrow Wilson. Similarly notable was the work of Olivier Zunz in *Making America Corporate, 1870–1920* (1990). By examining the creation of the what the Lynds called the "business class" in *Middletown*, Zunz opened exciting frontiers in social history that are in some ways similar to those initially explored by Thomas Cochran in his long and much-honored career.

The work of cultural historians has brought new perspectives and new life to the topic of the economic transformations covered in this book. Alan Trachtenberg, *The Incorporation of America* (1982) was a wide-ranging effort to understand the cultural implications of mechanization and the coming of giant corporations. Trachtenberg sought to explicate the "effects of the corporate system on culture, on values and outlooks, on the 'way of life.'" William Leach's 1993 study, *Land of Desire,* focused on the department store and the broad means through which a new culture of consumption came to dominate American society. Leach's work was imaginative, balanced, and highly critical of the corporate, consumer culture that accompanied the rise of big business. Like many such critics, he denied that Americans consented willingly to a new way of life organized around physical comfort and material well-being. He declared it "among the most nonconsensual public cultures ever created," despite the relatively rapid enthusiasm with which so many ordinary citizens and so many other institutions besides business embraced it. The work of Jackson Lears, especially his 1994 *Fables of Abundance,* explored the many dimensions of advertising's relationships to American culture, even to American consciousness. Another severe critic of corporate America, Lears lamented that business acquired after 1890 "the power to project a vision of the good life and make it prevail," thus giving the corporation "the most decisive power of all." Cultural perspectives even penetrated the *Cambridge Economic History of the United States: The Long Nineteenth Century* (2000), in a fine essay by Stuart Blumin on "The Social Implications of U.S. Economic Development." There remains much to be gained from the cultural approach.

The issue of whether or not Americans consented to the triumph of corporate, consumer capitalism has been strongly disputed. An early argument that they did not do so but were seduced by advertisers came in Stuart Ewen's *Captains of Consciousness: Advertising and the Social Roots of the Consumer Culture* (1976). Regina Blaszczyk's *Imagining Consumers* (2000) took a very different view, emphasizing the power of consumers in shaping the choices offered by business. Peter N. Stearns, *Consumerism in World History* (2002) traced the influence of consumer culture around the world and found its beginnings in eighteenth-century Britain and Europe. Others have seen its faint origins as early as the Renaissance.

The relationship of business to the history of women and minorities has attracted growing attention in recent years, subjects that long received relatively little attention. Wendy Gamber's 1997 study of *The Female Economy: The Millinery and Dressmaking Trades, 1860–1930,* is a rich example of the promise of this scholarship. Though there have been many contributors, the work of Angel Kwolek-Folland has been central to improving our understanding of women in business. Her 1994 study, *Engendering Business: Men and Women in the Corporate Office, 1870–1930,* and her wider work, *Incorporating Women: A History of Women and Business in the United States* (1998) did much to focus attention on this topic. Lynn Catanese's *Women's History: A Guide to Sources at Hagley Museum and Library* (1997) illustrated the wide range of research sources on this subject available in a major repository for American business history. The literature on race and business is substantial but fragmentary; the bibliography in Kwolek-Folland's *Incorporating Women* provides a good beginning point.

And it is clear that the topic of the political implications of the rise of big business can never be exhausted. That, as we have seen, was the first focus of historians' interest in the appearance and consequences of the modern corporation and concentration in industry. Thomas K. McCraw's thoughtful and gracefully written *Prophets of Regulation* (1984) was a reminder of the unanswered questions that remain concerning just how people learned to live with and shape the behavior of the enormous corporations that dominate modern life in the United States as well as in much of the rest of the world. Louis Galambos and Joseph Pratt, *The Rise of the Corporate Commonwealth: U.S. Business and Public Policy in the Twentieth Century* (1988) pointed to the criticisms of "the inflexibility and inefficiency of American business and political institutions" that began in the 1970s, reviewed the history of such institutions since the days of J. P. Morgan, and argued that the system was and remained resilient and capable of responding to its difficulties. The more recent work of the political critics of big business such as Neil Fligstein, William Roy, Charles Perrow, et al., discussed above, shows the continuing power of this subject.

The economic, technological, and social triumph of big business and its subsequent increasingly global scope have done much to homogenize our world. Even the nation state itself has become less powerful as many decisions of global impact are taken in the headquarters of international corporations and not in the halls of government. The highly visible economic success of the giant industrial enterprise, whether in the United States, Germany, Britain, France, Japan, or elsewhere, has flowed from and reinforced an apparent notion in the developed world that the primary purpose of life is material gain. Much, indeed most, of the world's population has yet to enjoy the full fruits of industrial progress, and as more populations do so, ecological problems will likely multiply. But as societies and scholars struggle to understand these cultural transformations, they will do so with the benefit of a reasonably coherent historical picture of the emergence of big business, industrial capitalism, and industrial society. It is a picture that has resulted from the work of the numerous historians of business, economic change, technology, law, labor, gender, and culture. As our circumstances shift, the questions we ask of the past and the answers we draw from it will surely continue to evolve. Interest in the rise of big business, however, seems likely to endure.

INDEX

The Rise of Big Business, 1860–1920, Third Edition
Developmental editor and Copy editor: Andrew J. Davidson
Production editor: Lucy Herz
Proofreader: Claudia Siler
Indexer: Pat Rimmer
Printer: Versa Press, Inc.